# World War II Airplanes

## Coloring Book for Adults 1 & 2

D1737483

ColoringArtist.com

**Vought F4U Corsair**

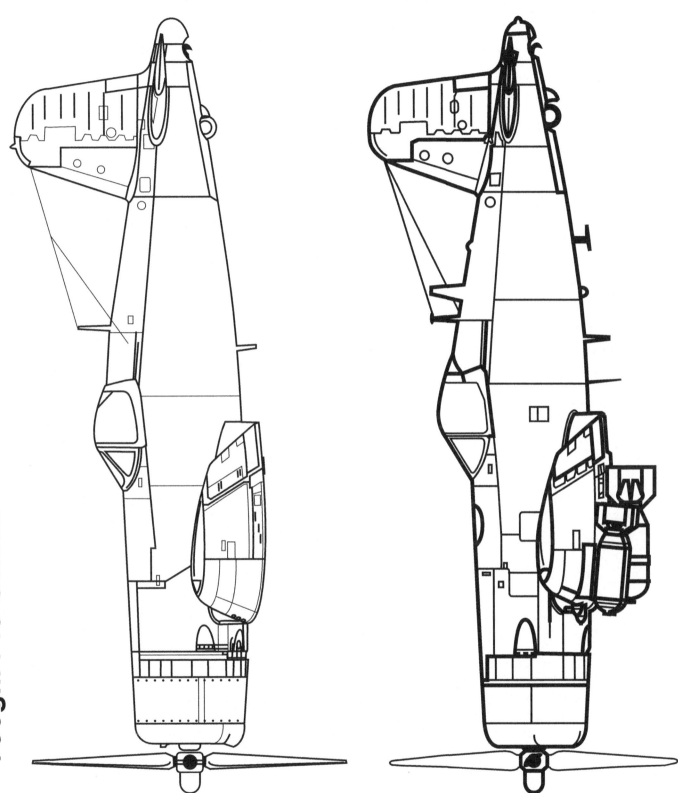

Grumman F4F Wildcat

ROYAL NAVY
AX 730

ROYAL NAVY
JW 792

**Hawker Tempest**

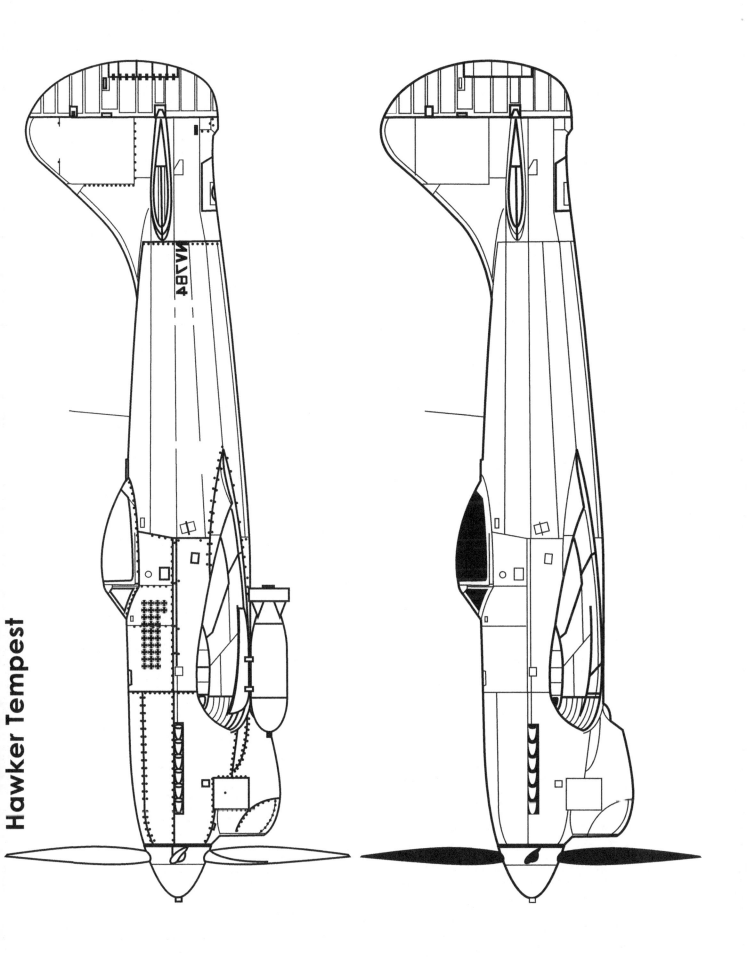

# Messerschmitt Bf 109

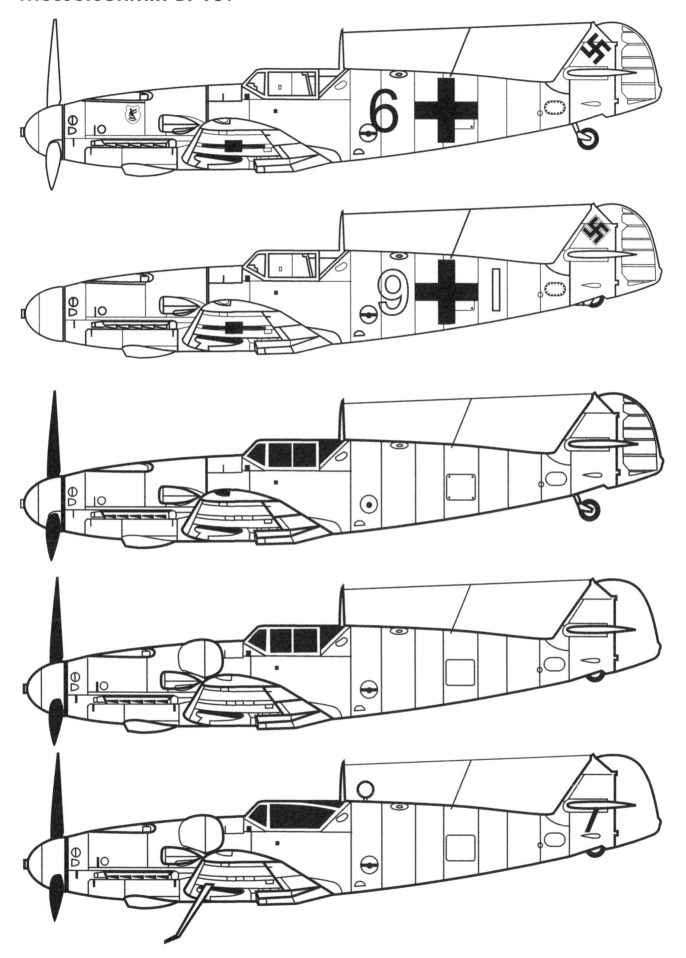

# Northrop P-61 Black Widow

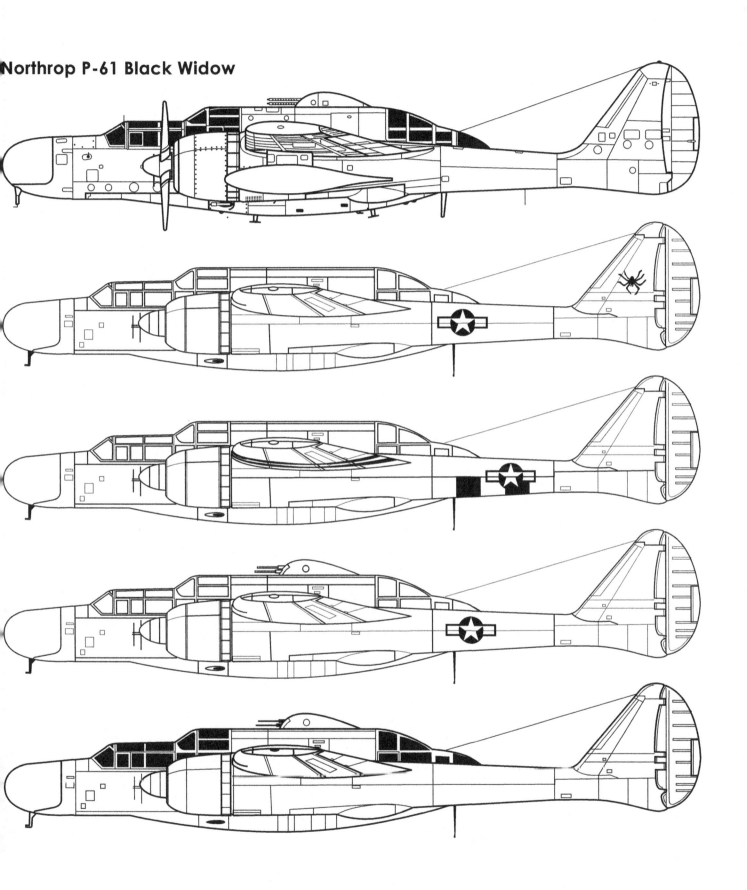

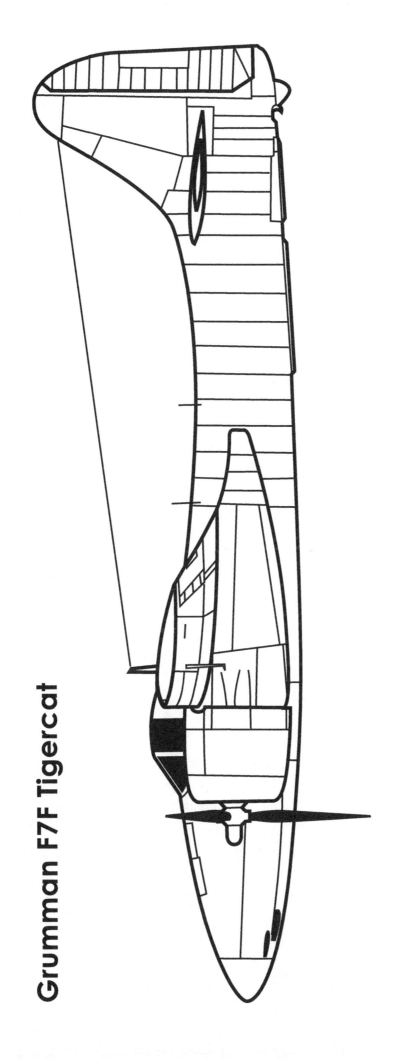

Grumman F7F Tigercat

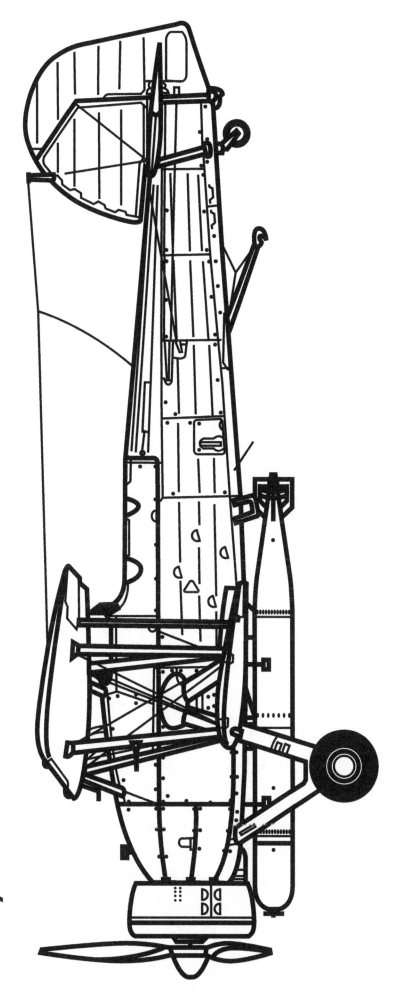

Fairey Swordfish

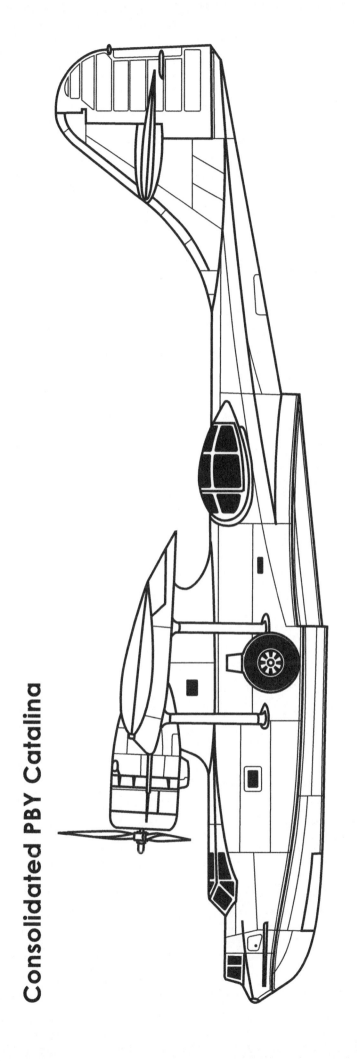

Consolidated PBY Catalina

Curtiss P-40 Warhawk

Hawker Typhoon

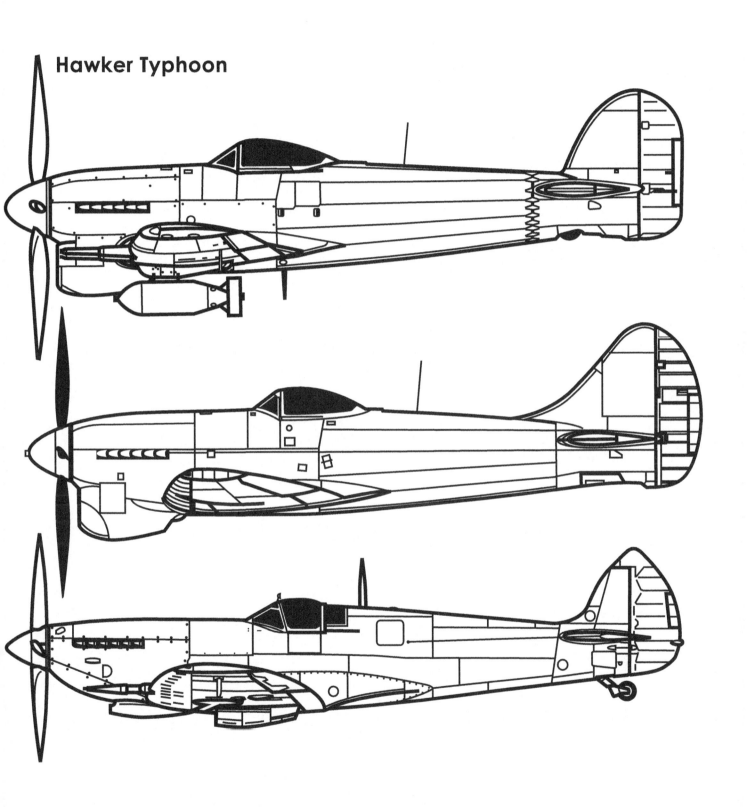

North American B-25 Mitchell

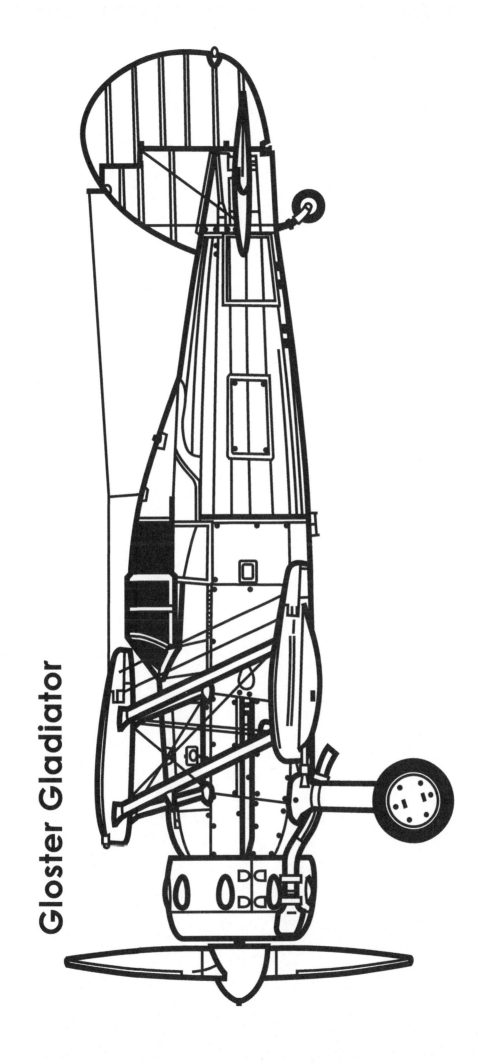

Gloster Gladiator

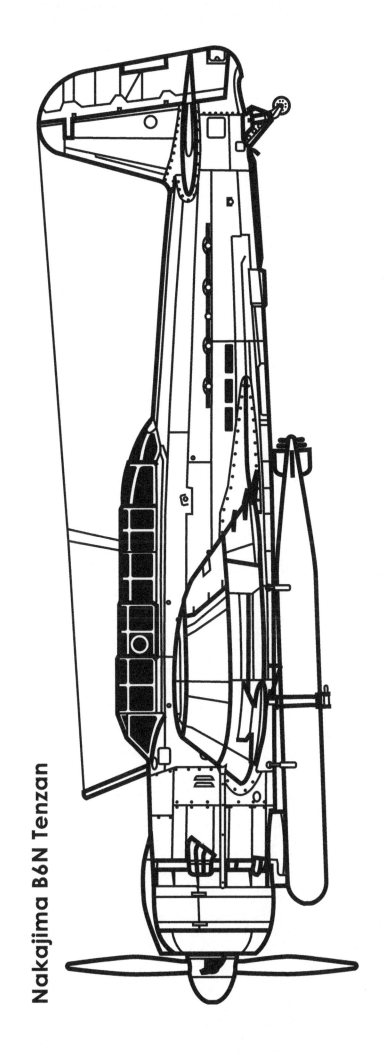

Nakajima B6N Tenzan

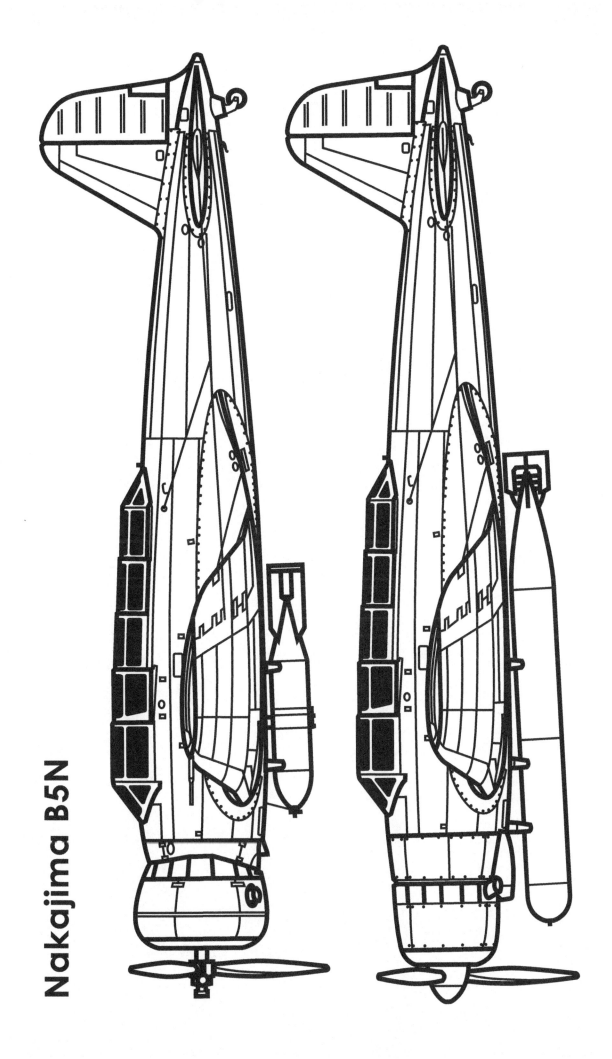

Nakajima B5N

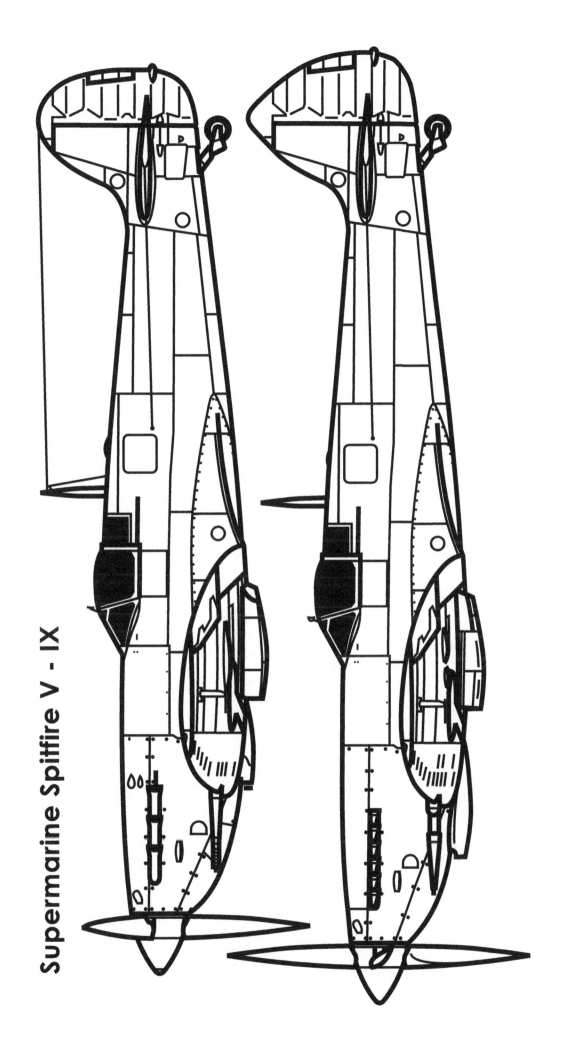

Supermarine Spitfire V - IX

Petlyakov Pe-2

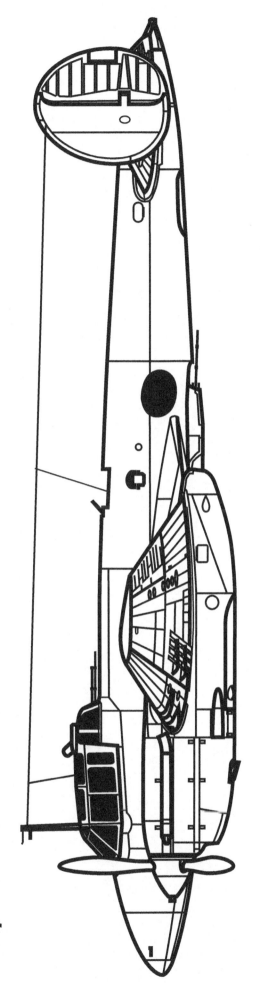

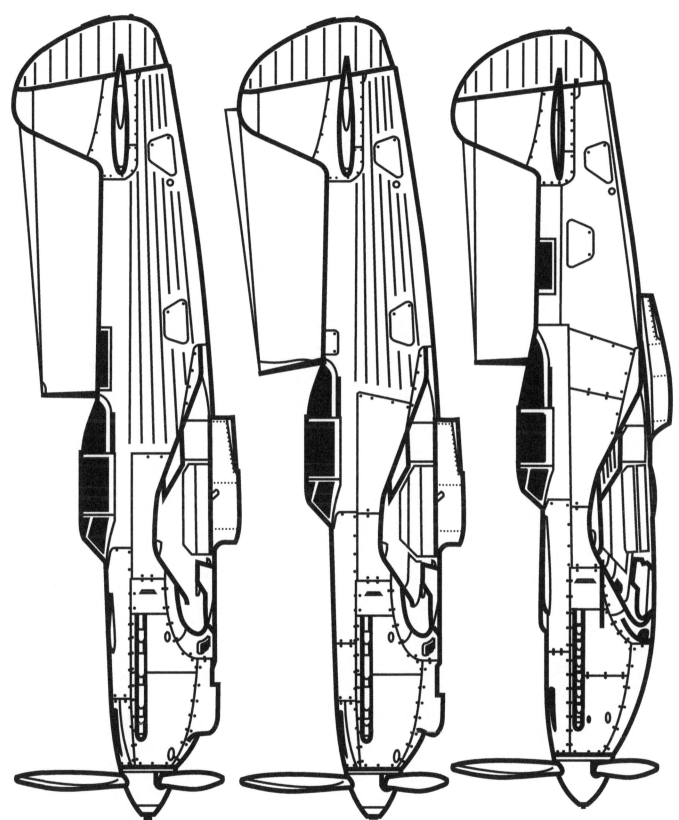

Yakovlev Yak-9

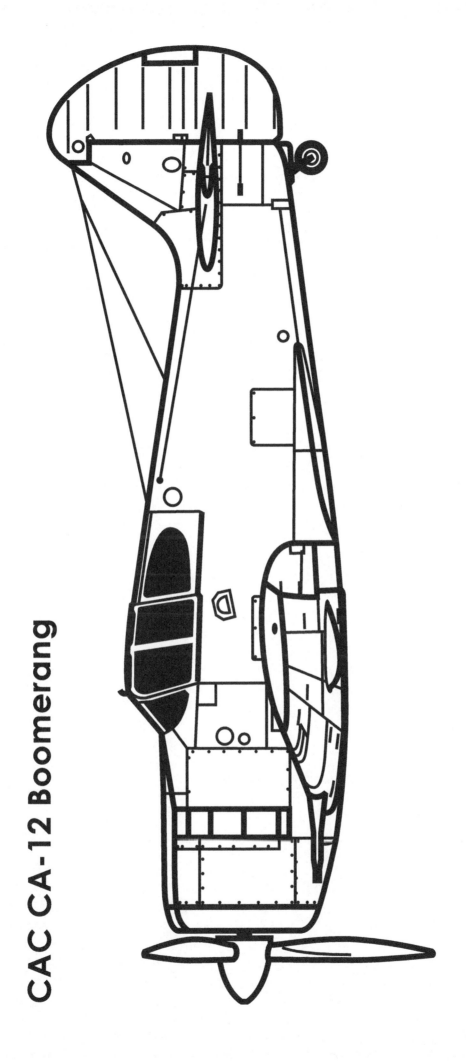

CAC CA-12 Boomerang

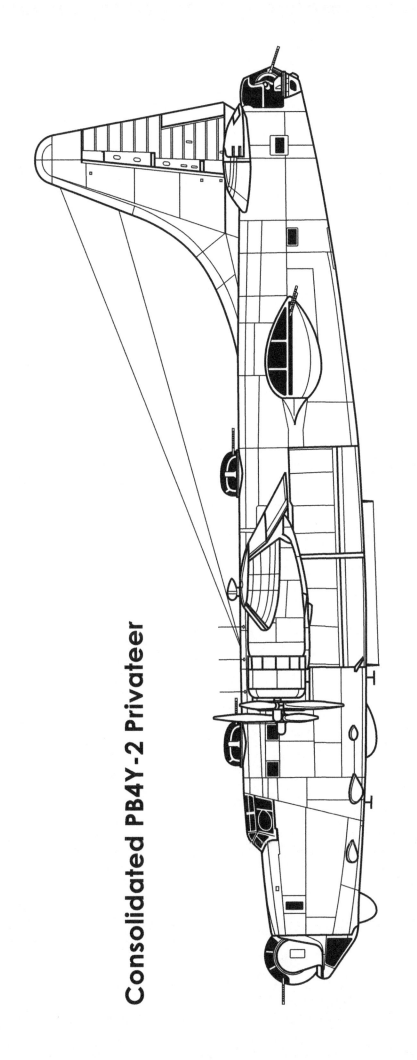

Consolidated PB4Y-2 Privateer

Vickers Wellington

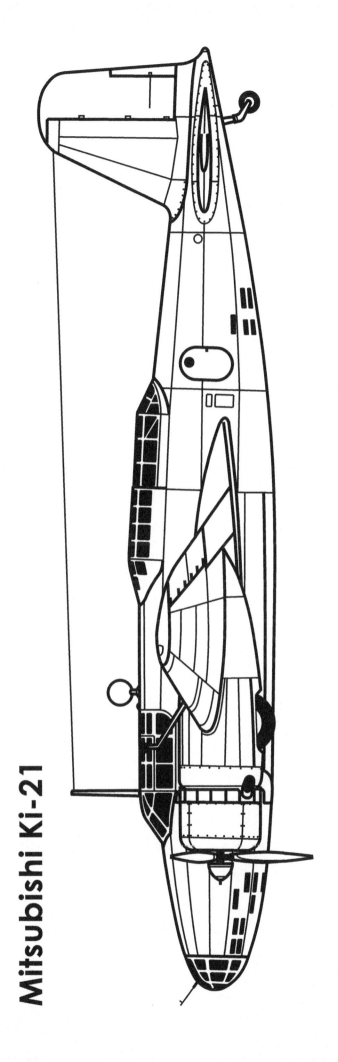

Mitsubishi Ki-21

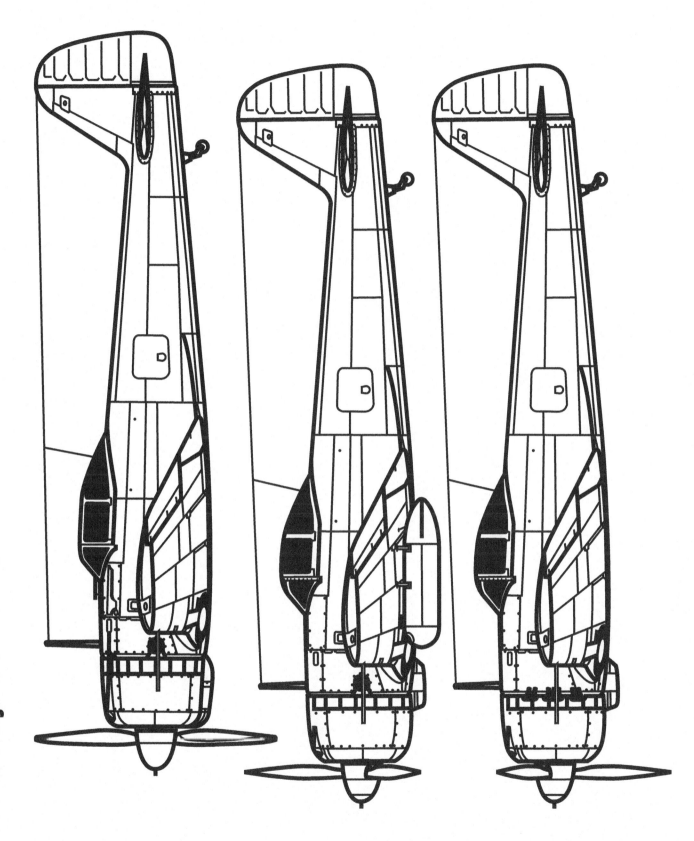

**Nakajima Ki-43**

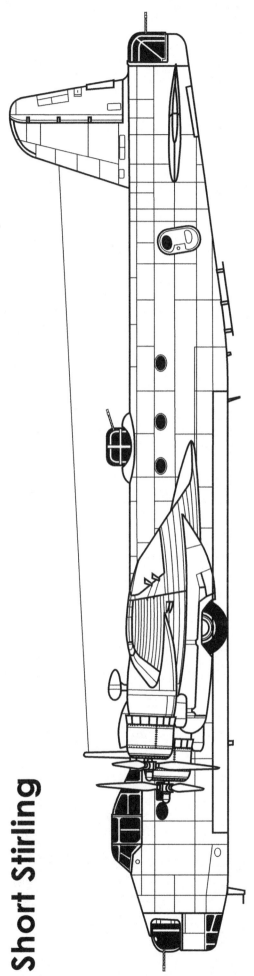

**Short Stirling**

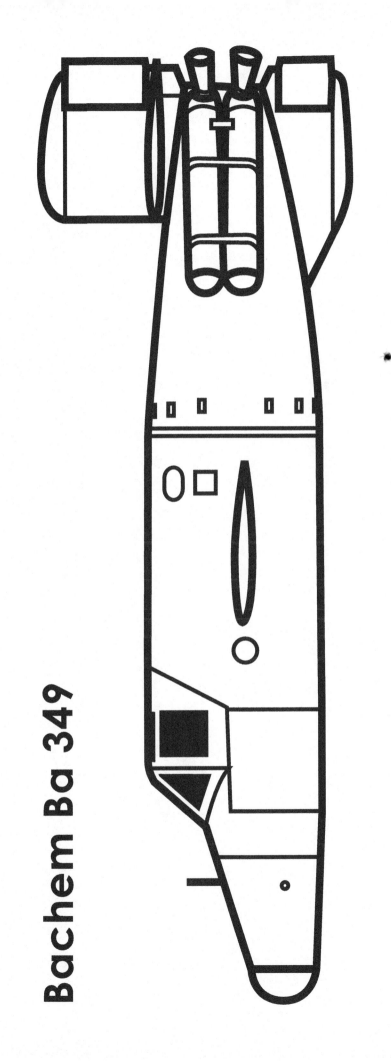

**Bachem Ba 349**

de Havilland Mosquito

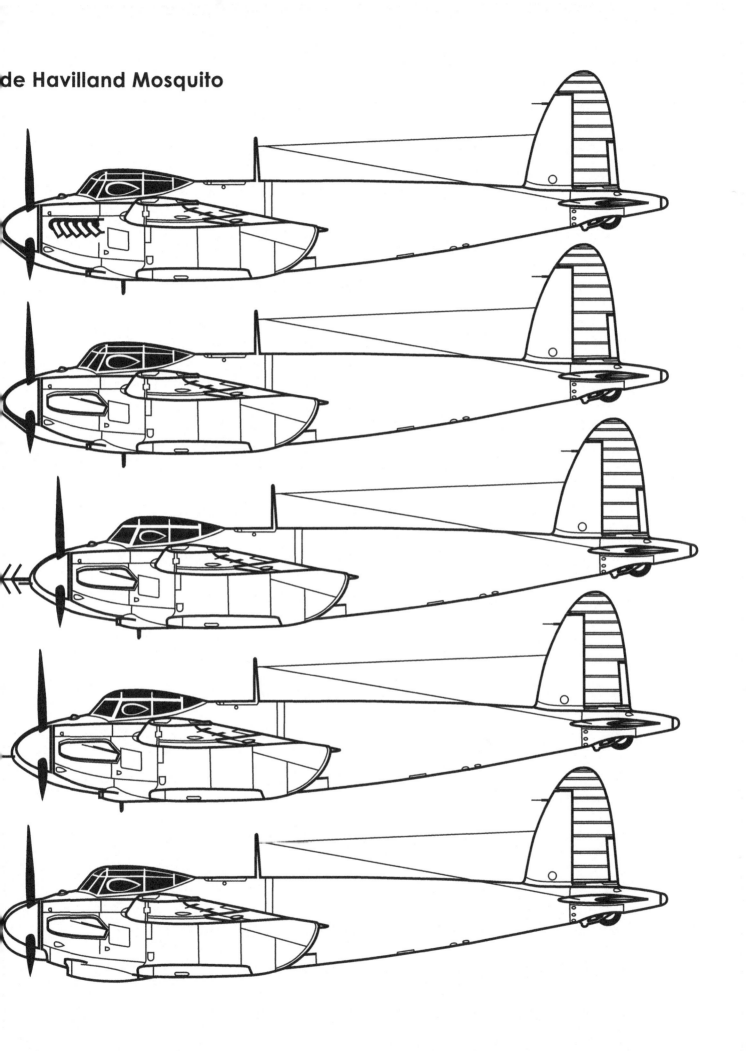

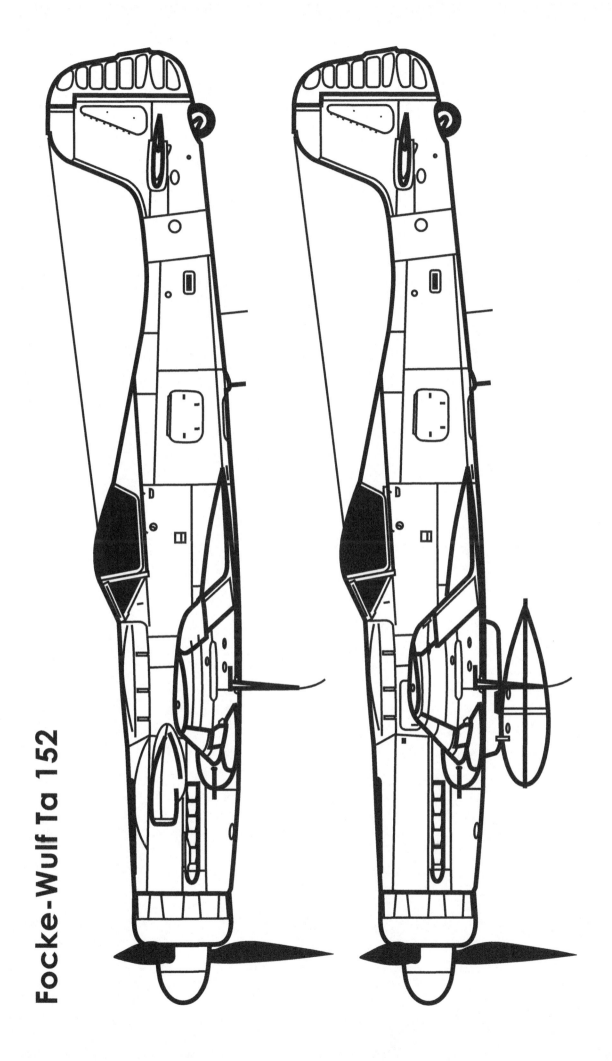

**Focke-Wulf Ta 152**

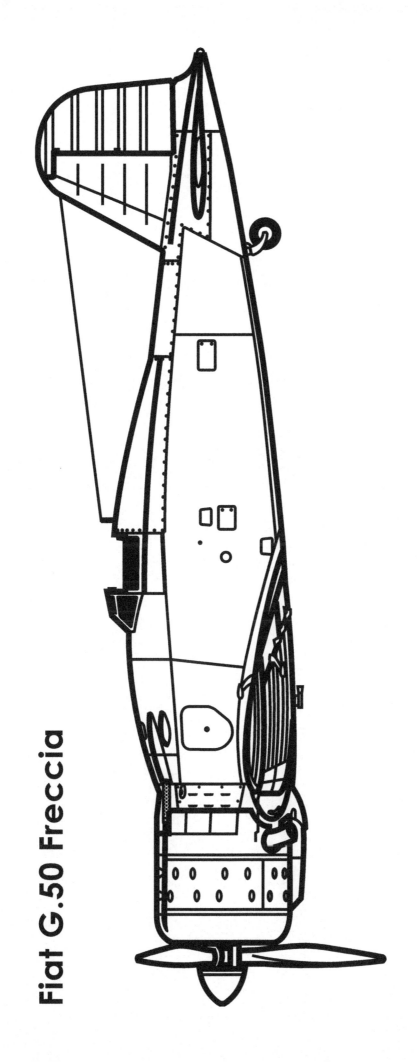

Fiat G.50 Freccia

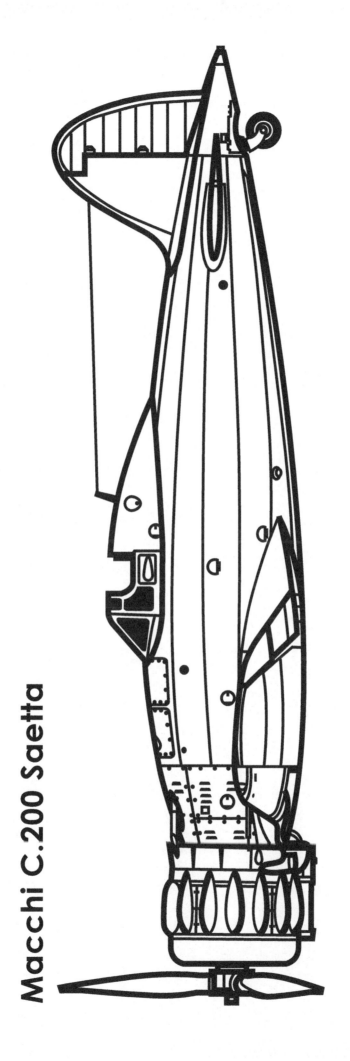

Macchi C.200 Saetta

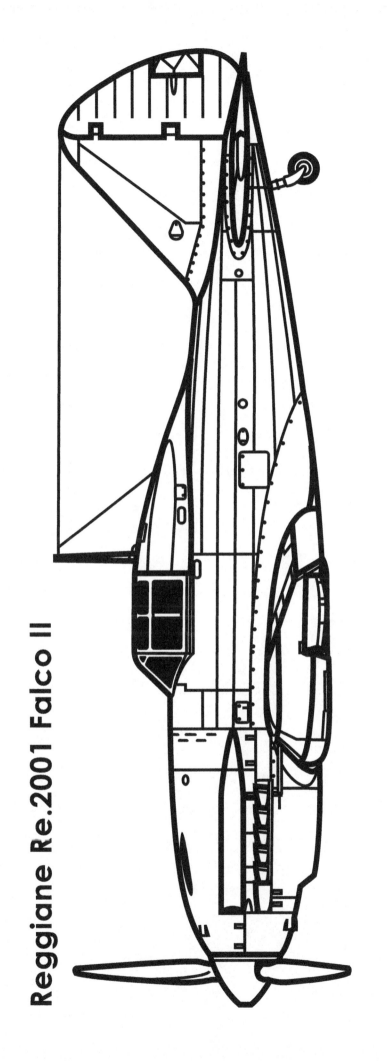

Reggiane Re.2001 Falco II

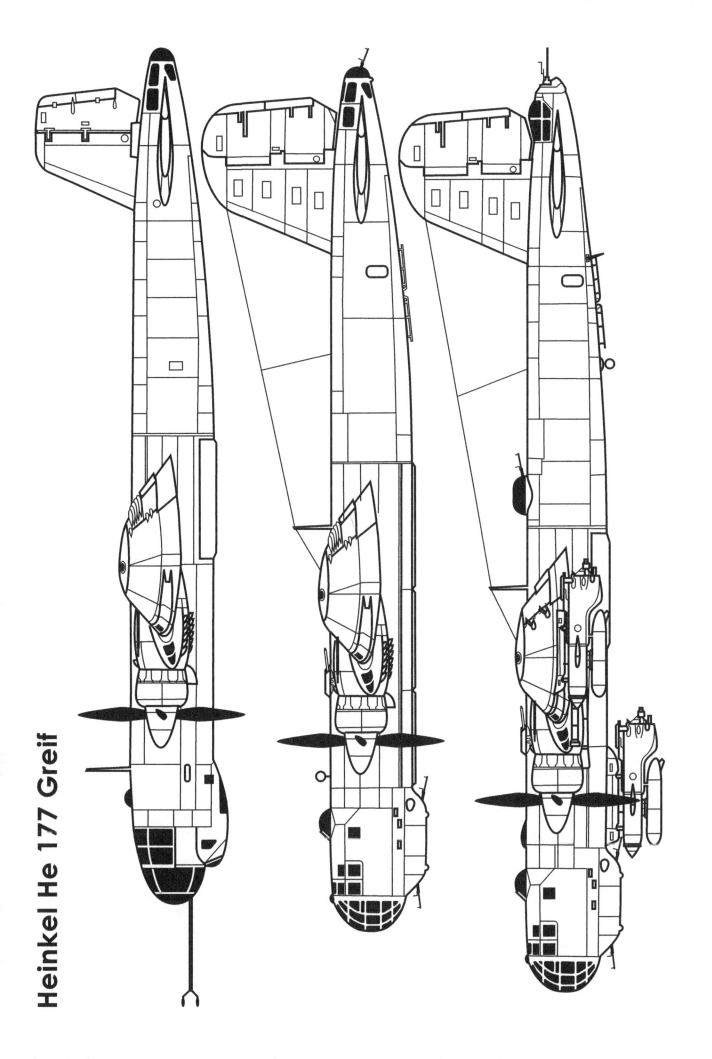

Heinkel He 177 Greif

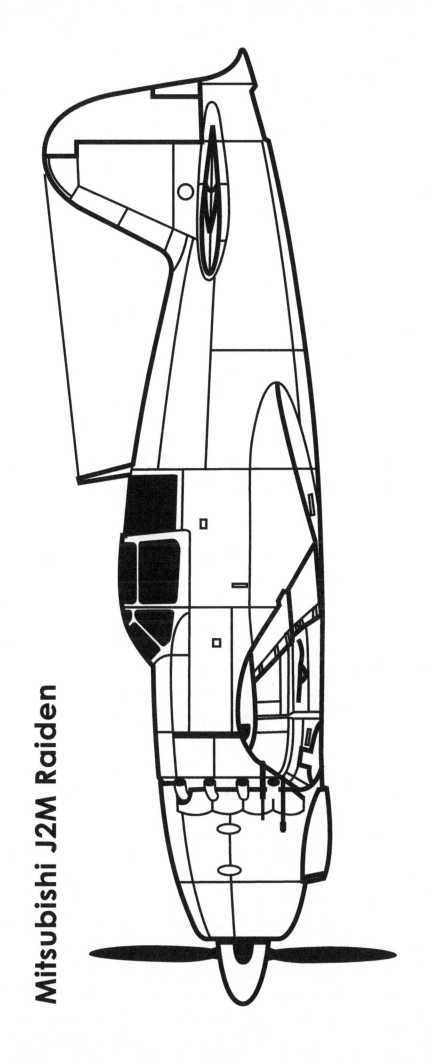

Mitsubishi J2M Raiden

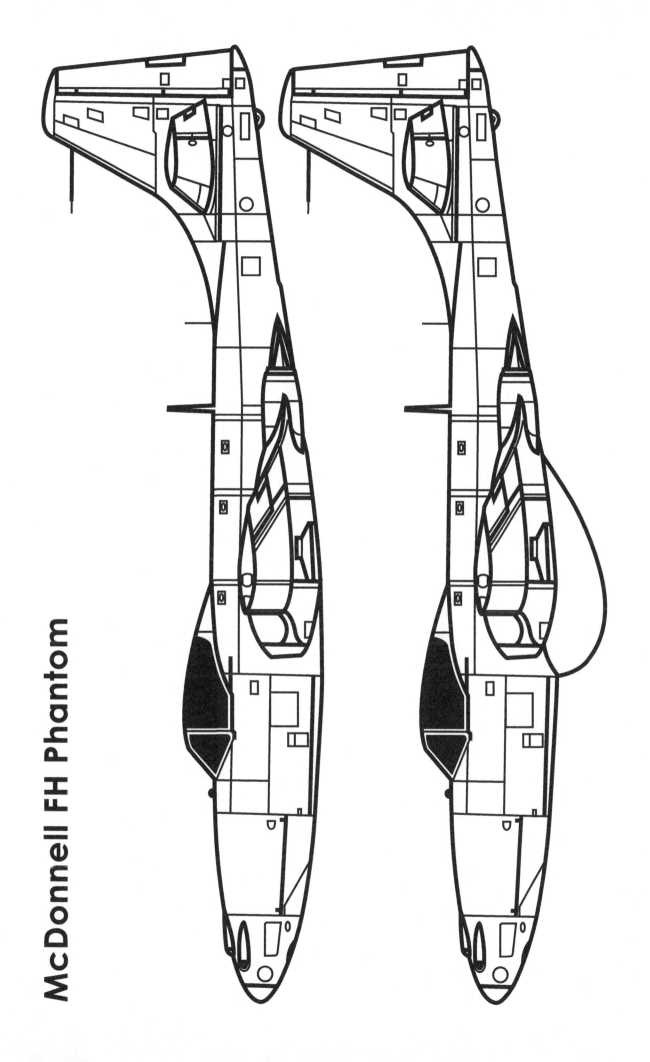

McDonnell FH Phantom

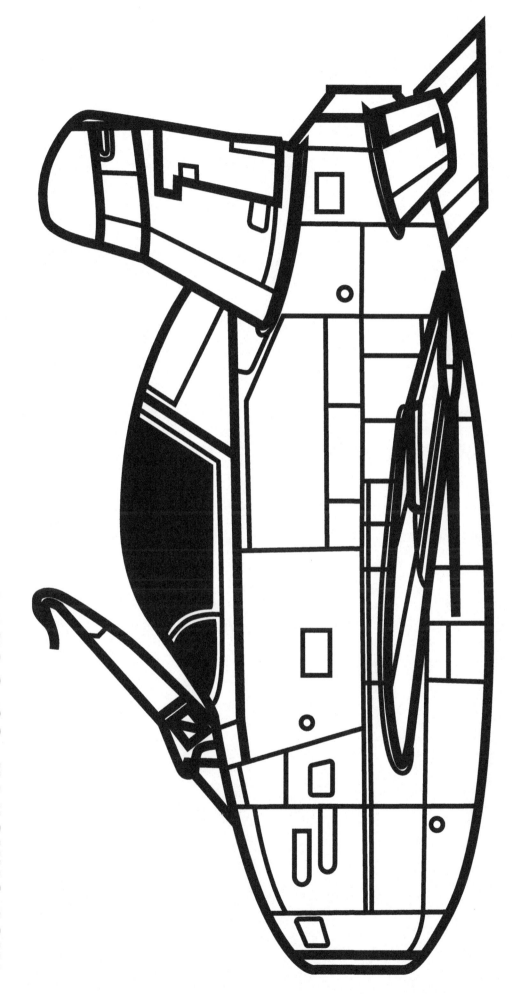

McDonnell XF-85 Goblin

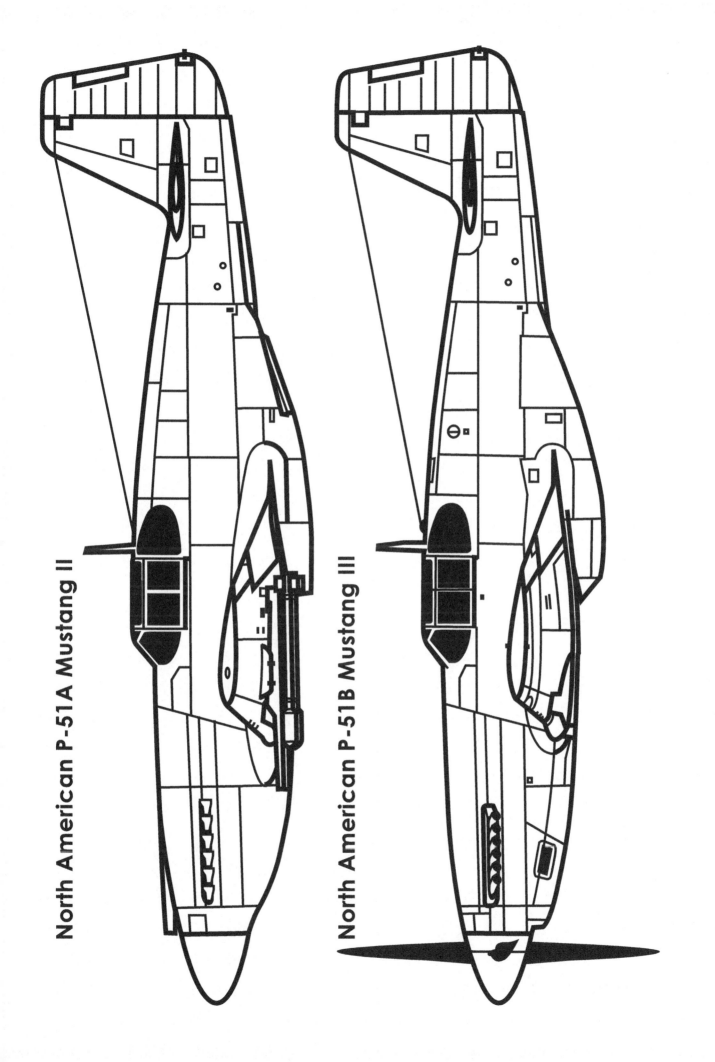

North American P-51A Mustang II

North American P-51B Mustang III

# Polikarpov I-15

# Polikarpov I-15bis

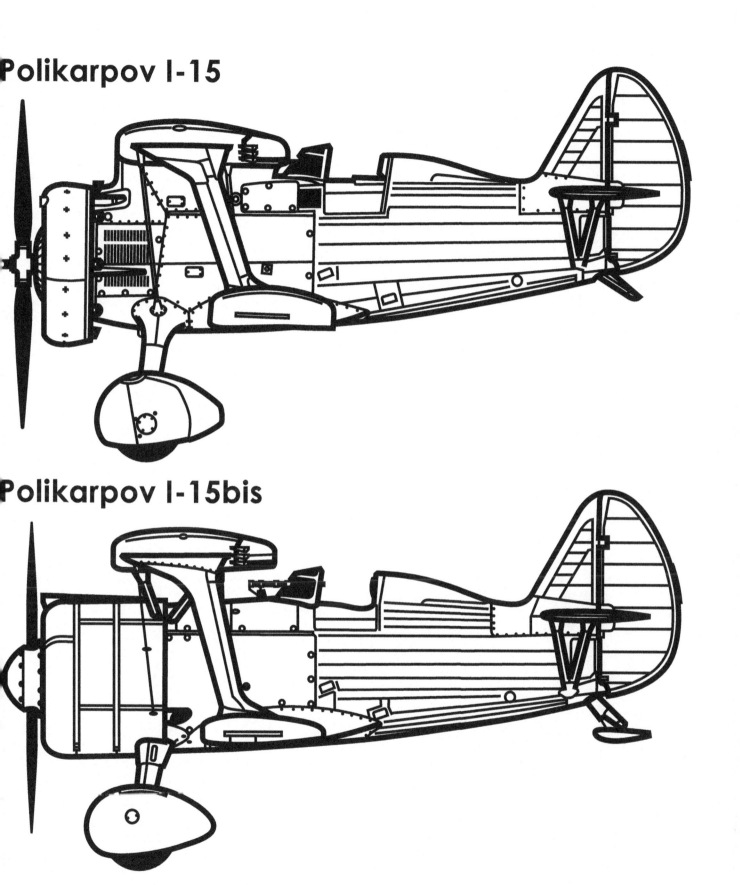

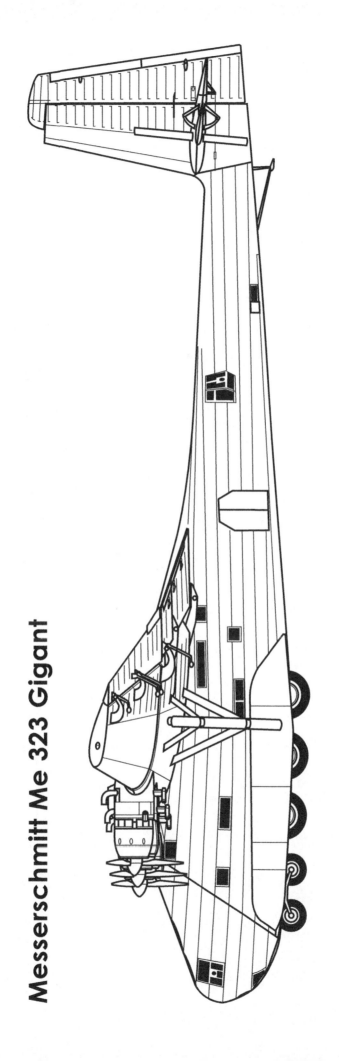

Messerschmitt Me 323 Gigant

Heinkel He 111

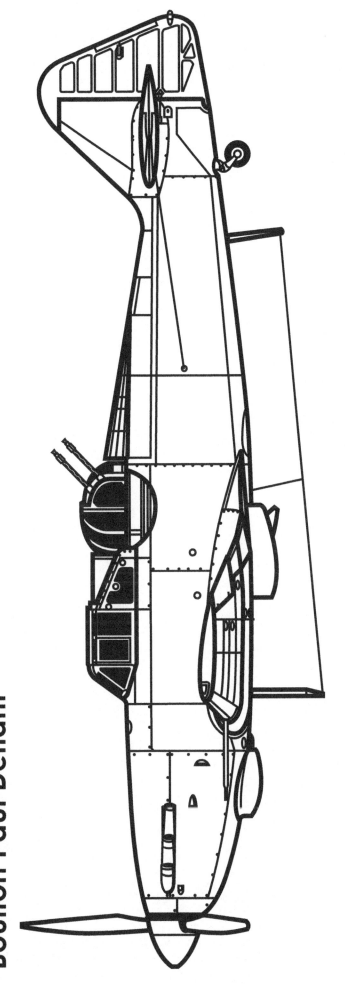

**Boulton Paul Defiant**

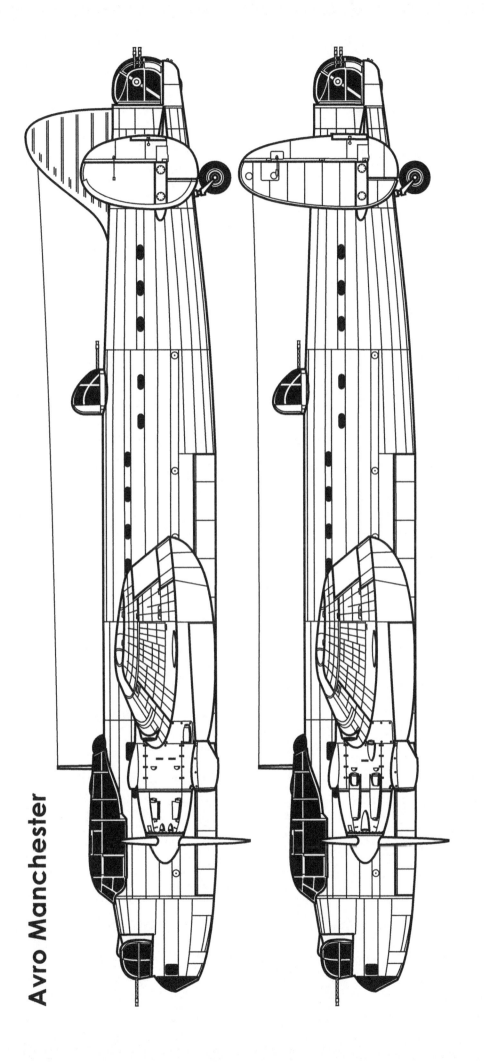

Avro Manchester

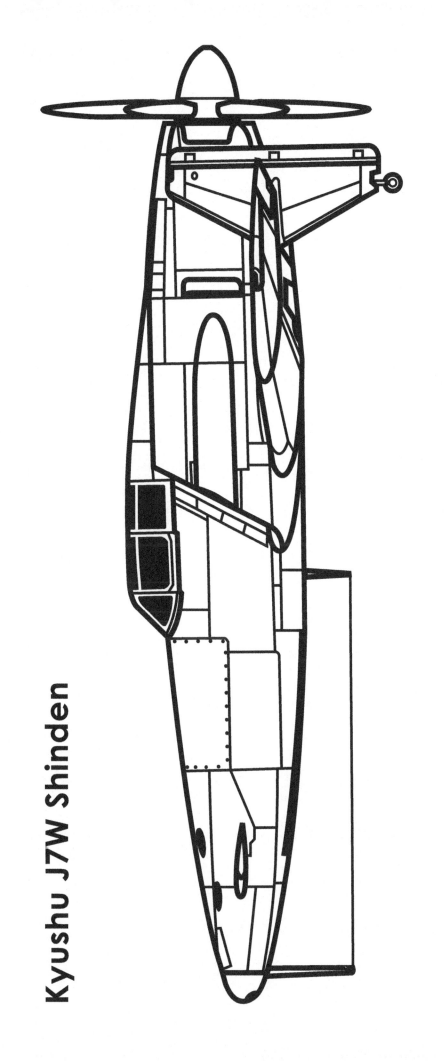

**Kyushu J7W Shinden**

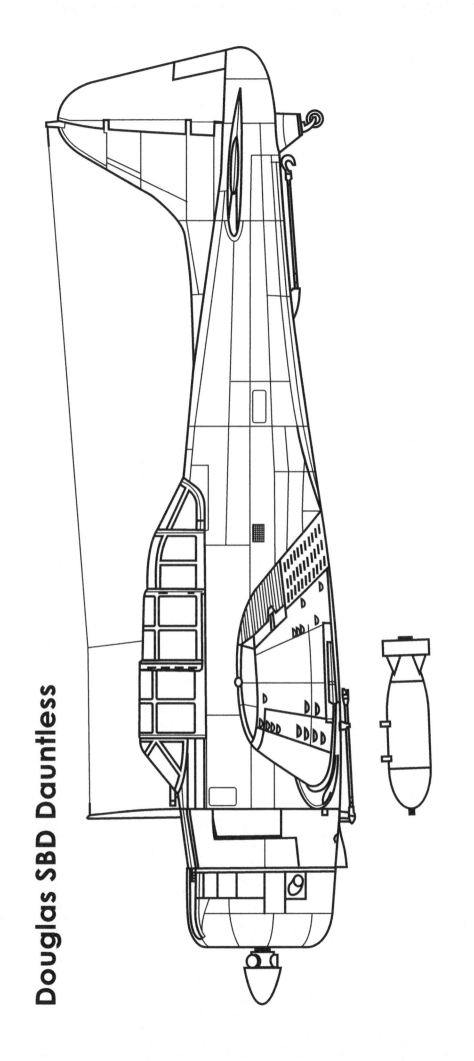

Douglas SBD Dauntless

# Grumman F6F Hellcat

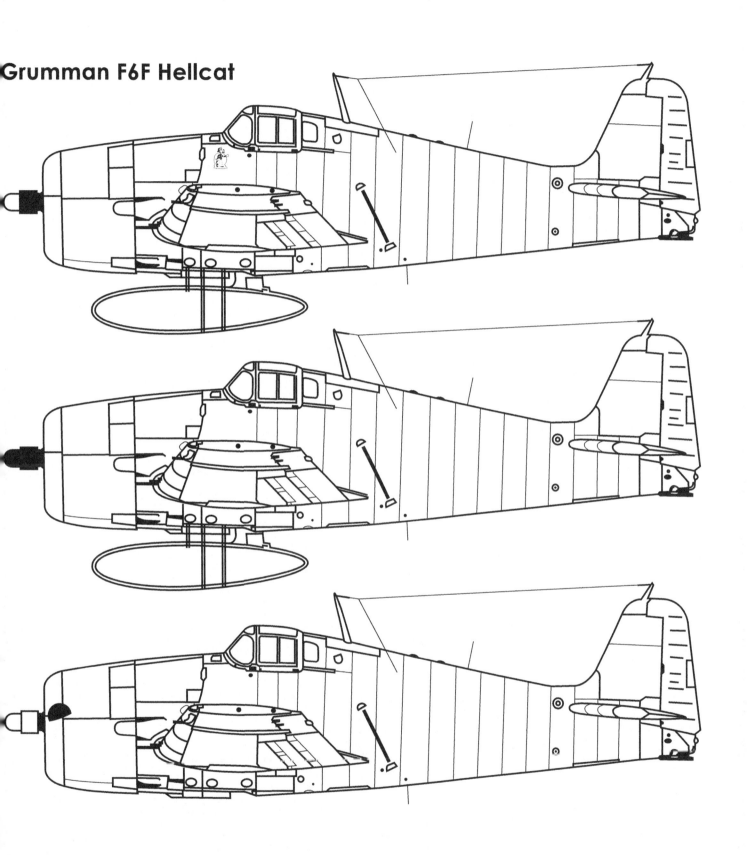

# Hawker Hurricane

# Hawker Hurricane MkI

# Hawker Hurricane MkIID

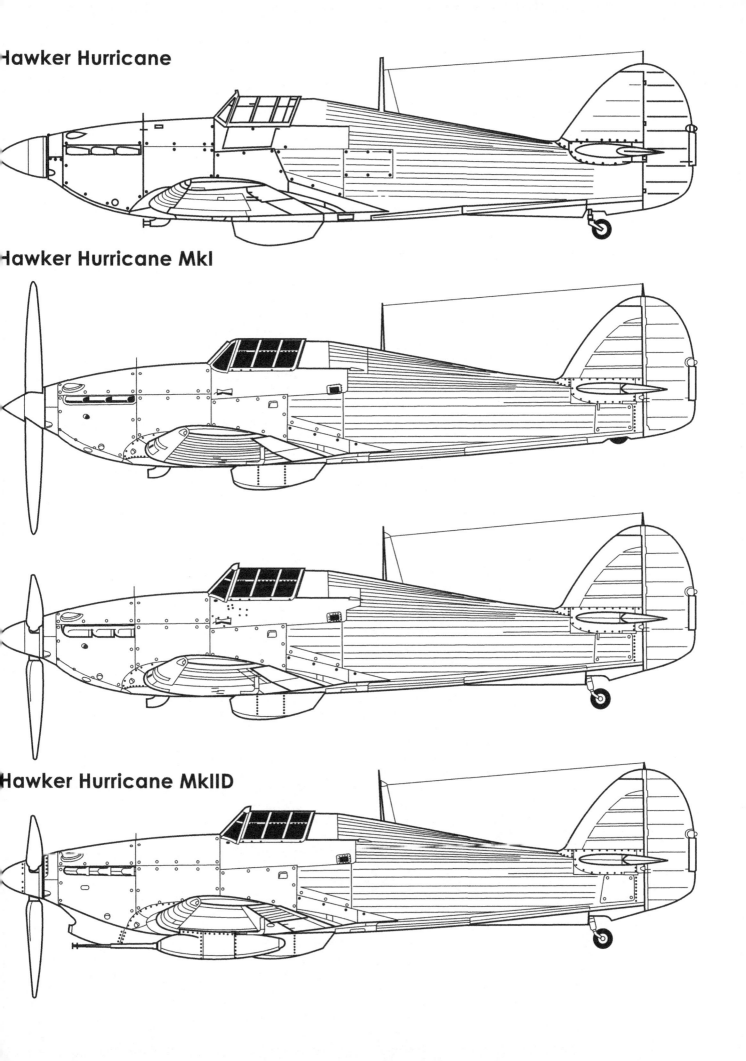

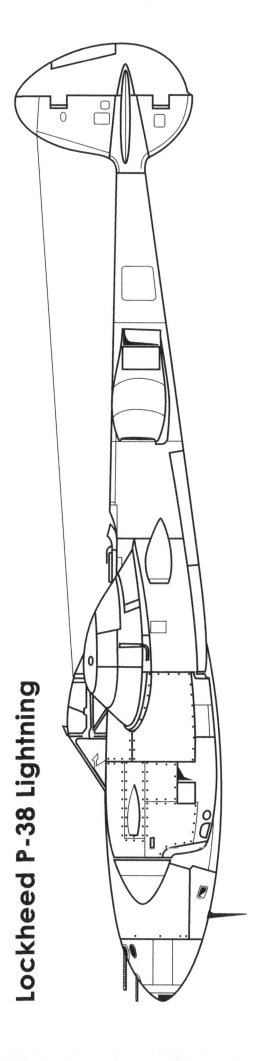

**Lockheed P-38 Lightning**

# North American P-51D Mustang

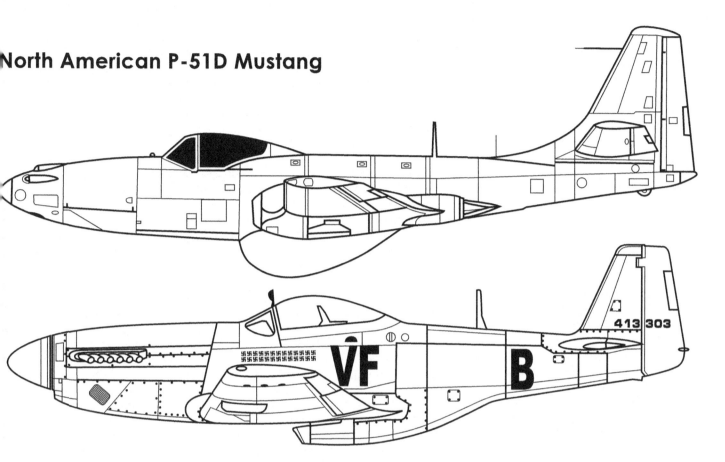

413303
VF B

# North American P-51D Mustang IV

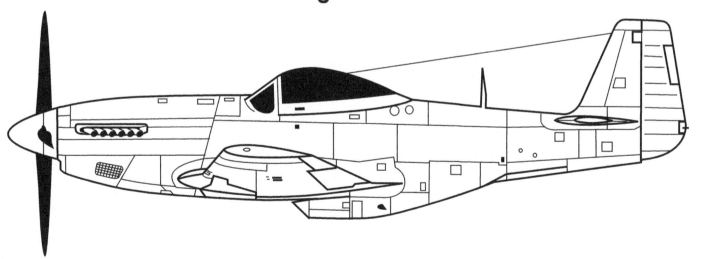

# Republic P-47 Thunderbolt

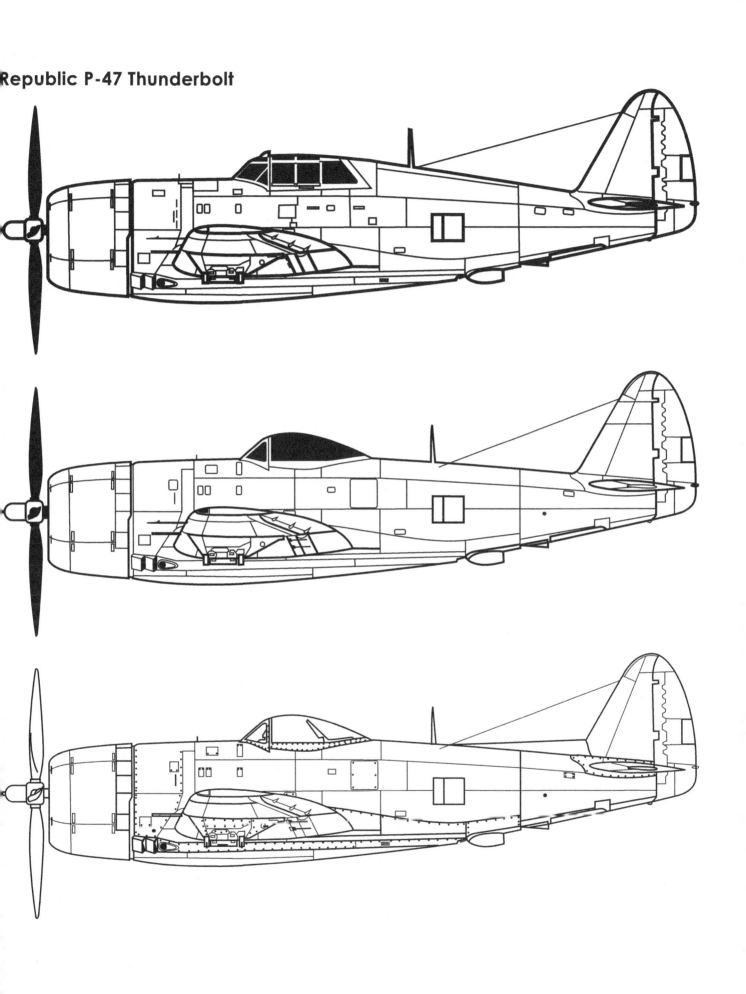

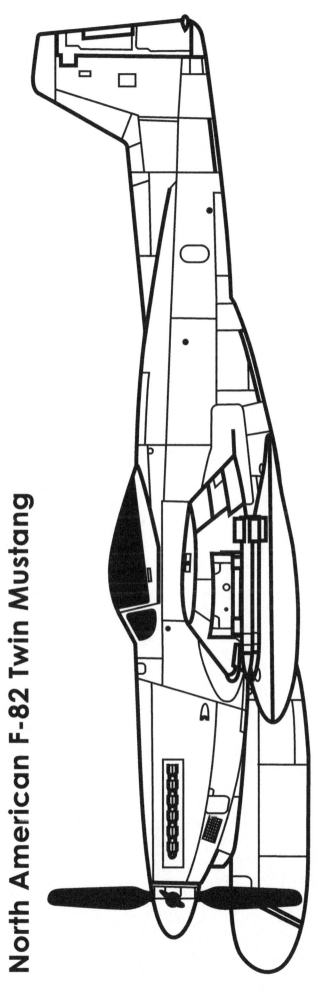

North American F-82 Twin Mustang

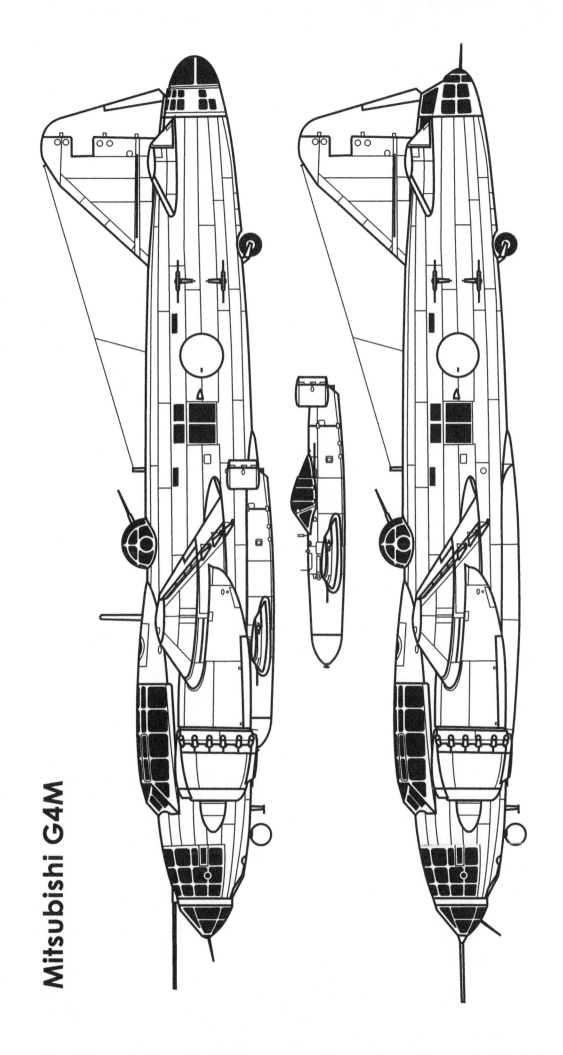

Mitsubishi G4M

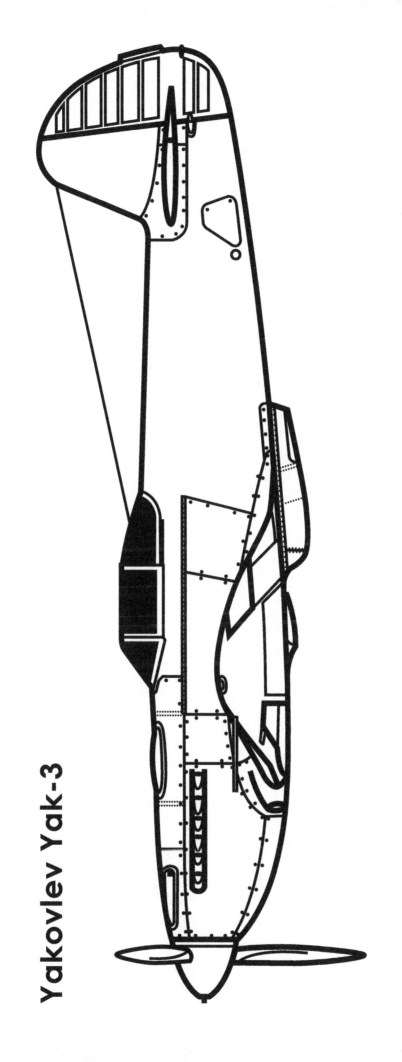

Yakovlev Yak-3

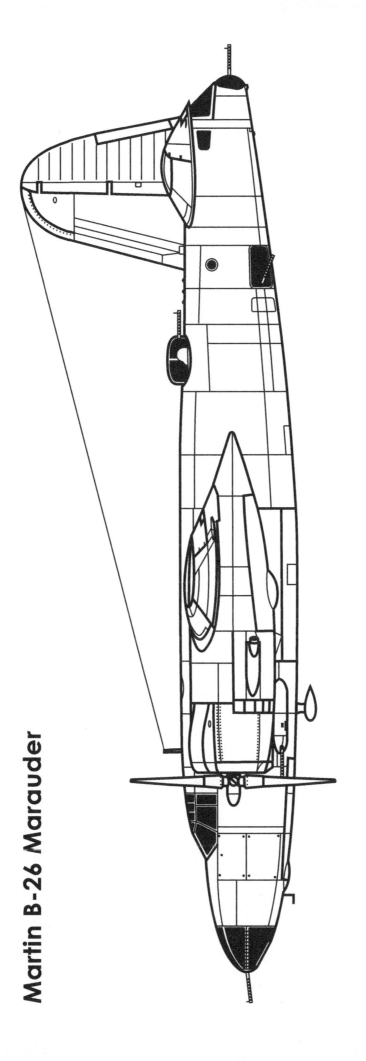

Martin B-26 Marauder

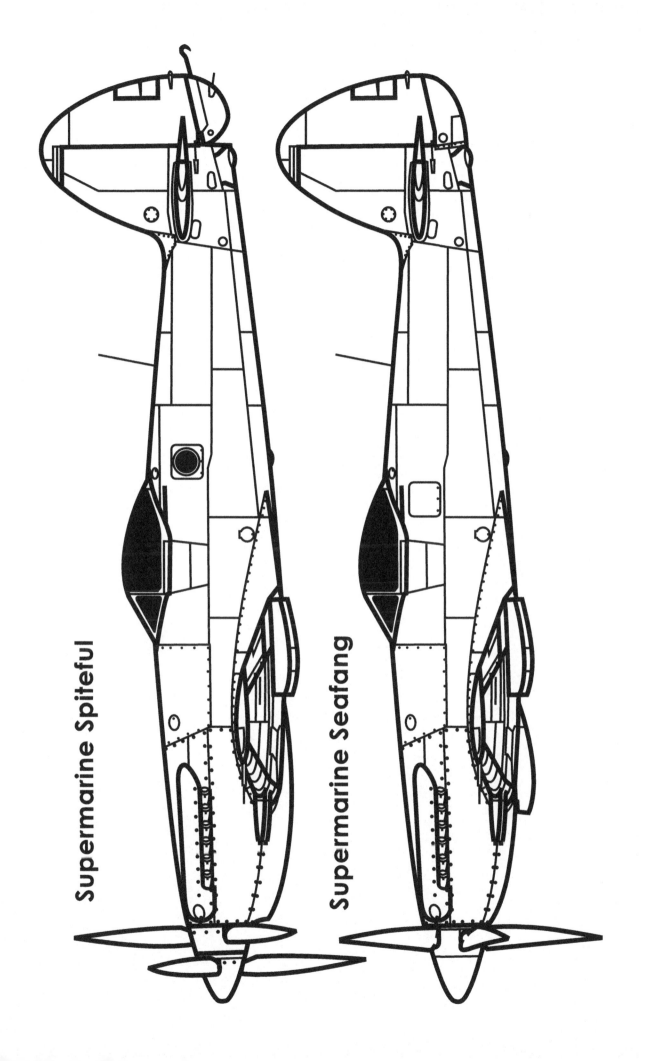

Supermarine Spiteful

Supermarine Seafang

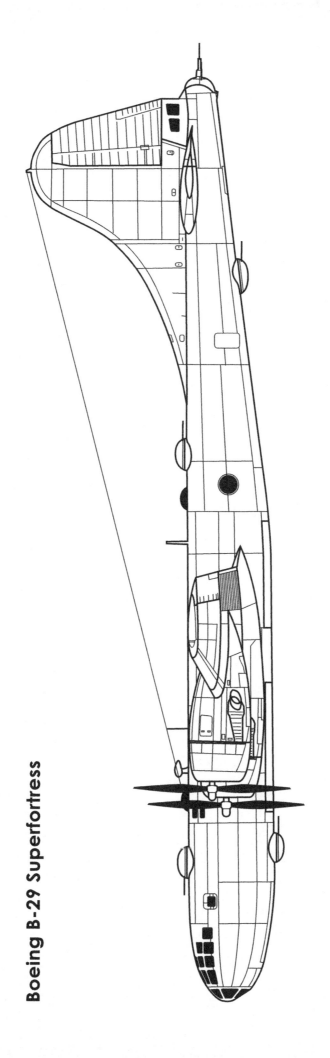

Boeing B-29 Superfortress

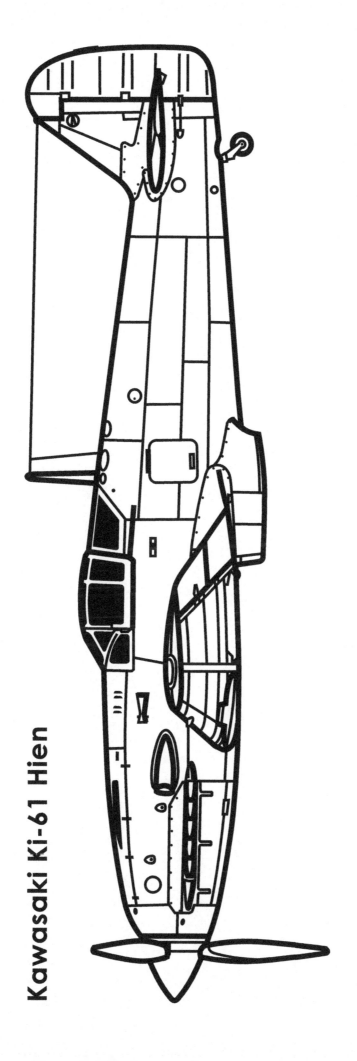

Kawasaki Ki-61 Hien

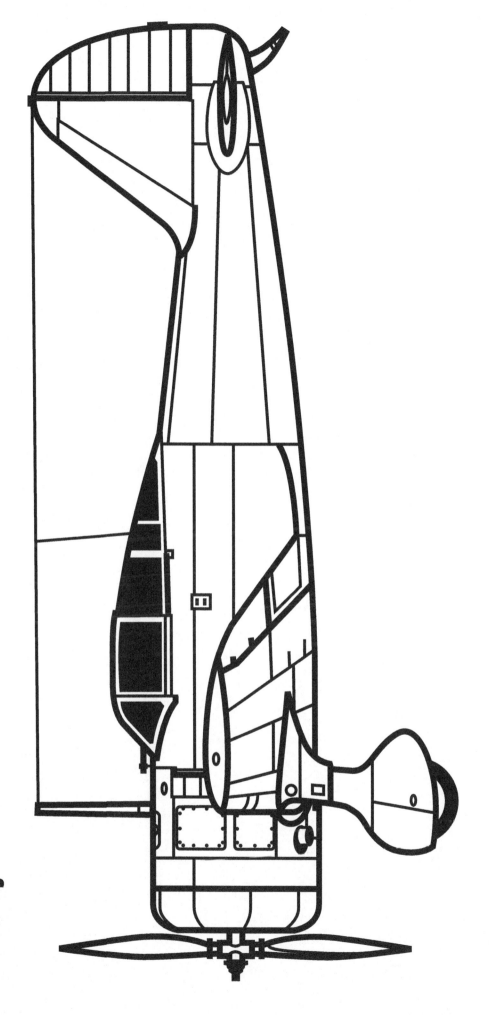

Nakajima Ki-27

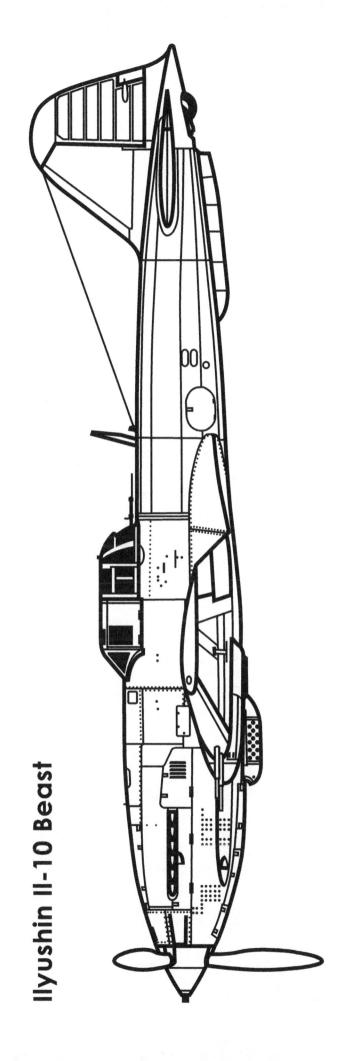

Ilyushin Il-10 Beast

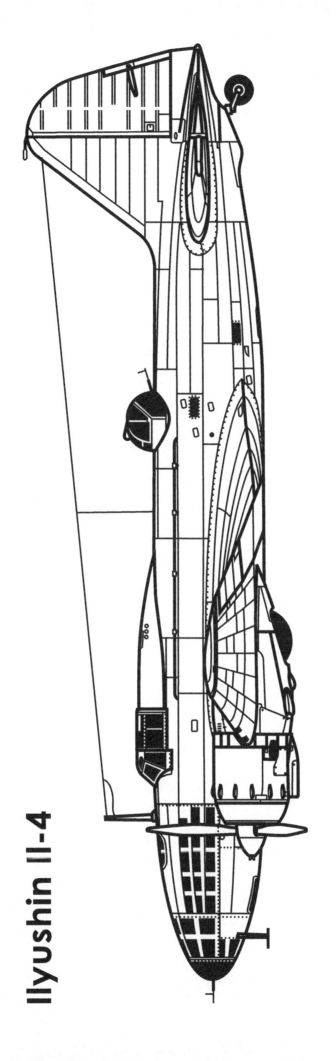

Ilyushin Il-4

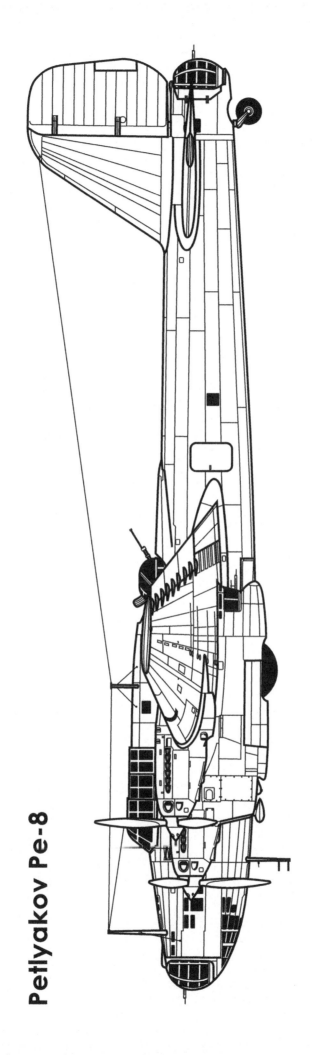

Petlyakov Pe-8

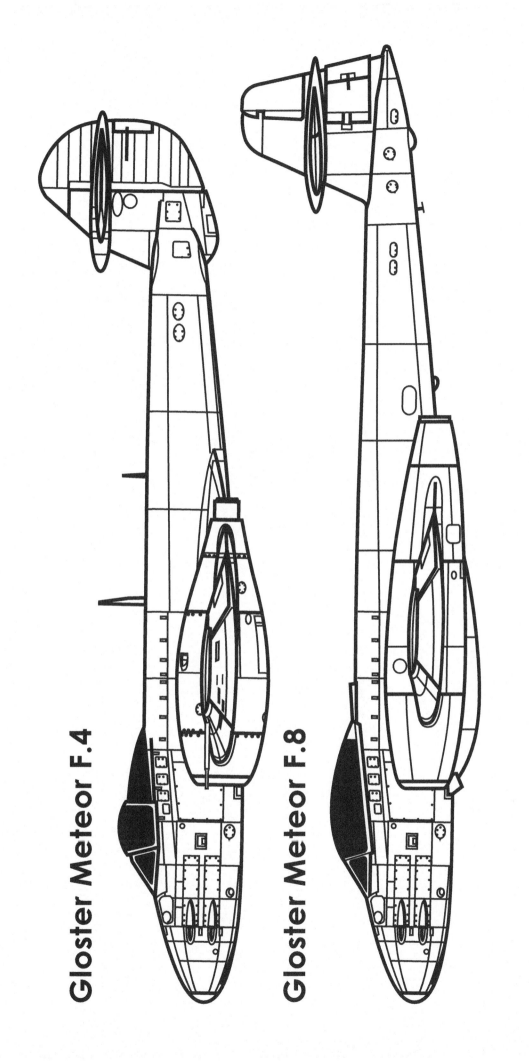

Gloster Meteor F.4

Gloster Meteor F.8

**Bristol Beaufighter**

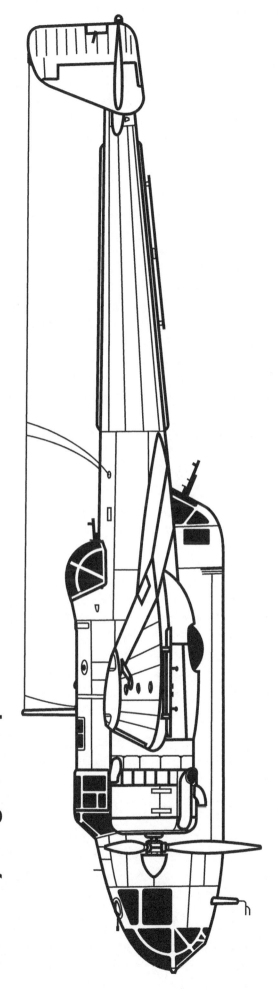

Handley Page Hampden

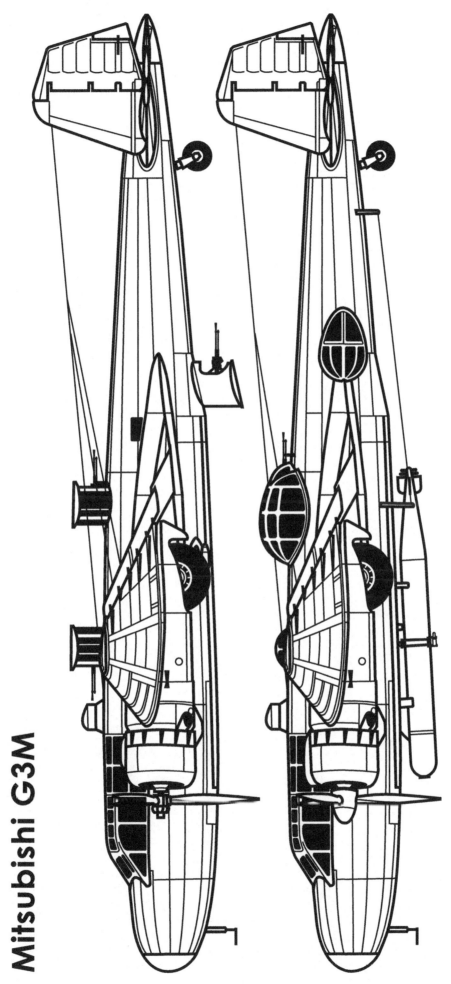

Mitsubishi G3M

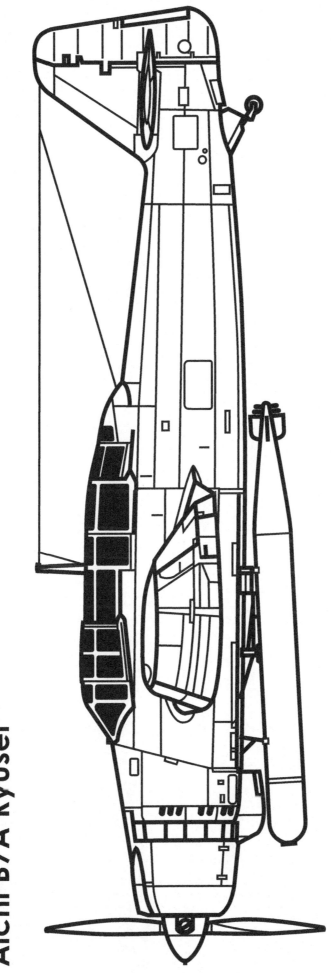

Aichi B7A Ryusei

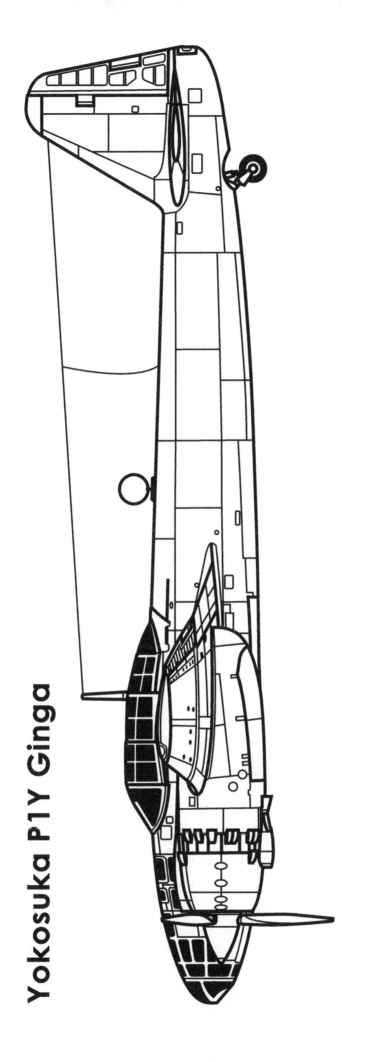

Yokosuka P1Y Ginga

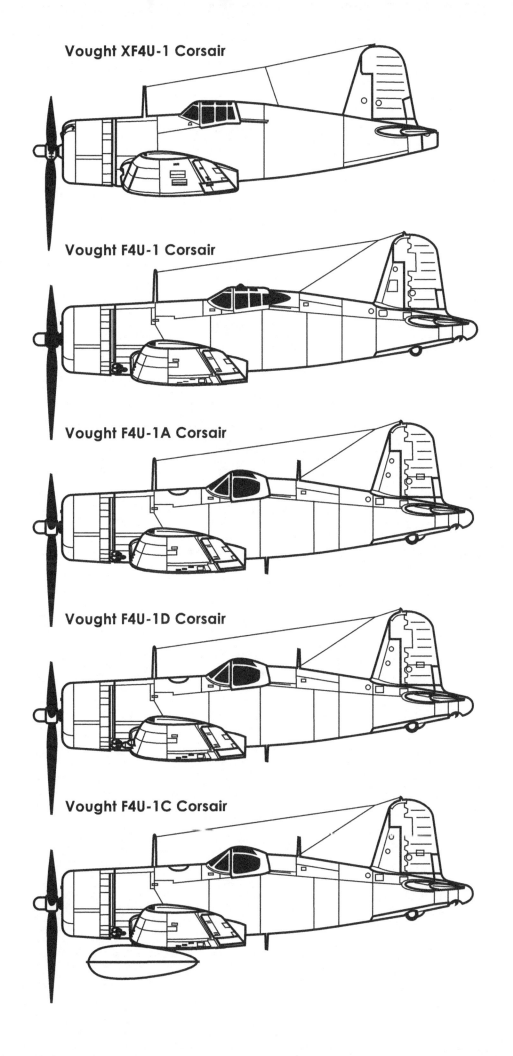

Vought XF4U-1 Corsair

Vought F4U-1 Corsair

Vought F4U-1A Corsair

Vought F4U-1D Corsair

Vought F4U-1C Corsair

## Consolidated B-24 Liberator

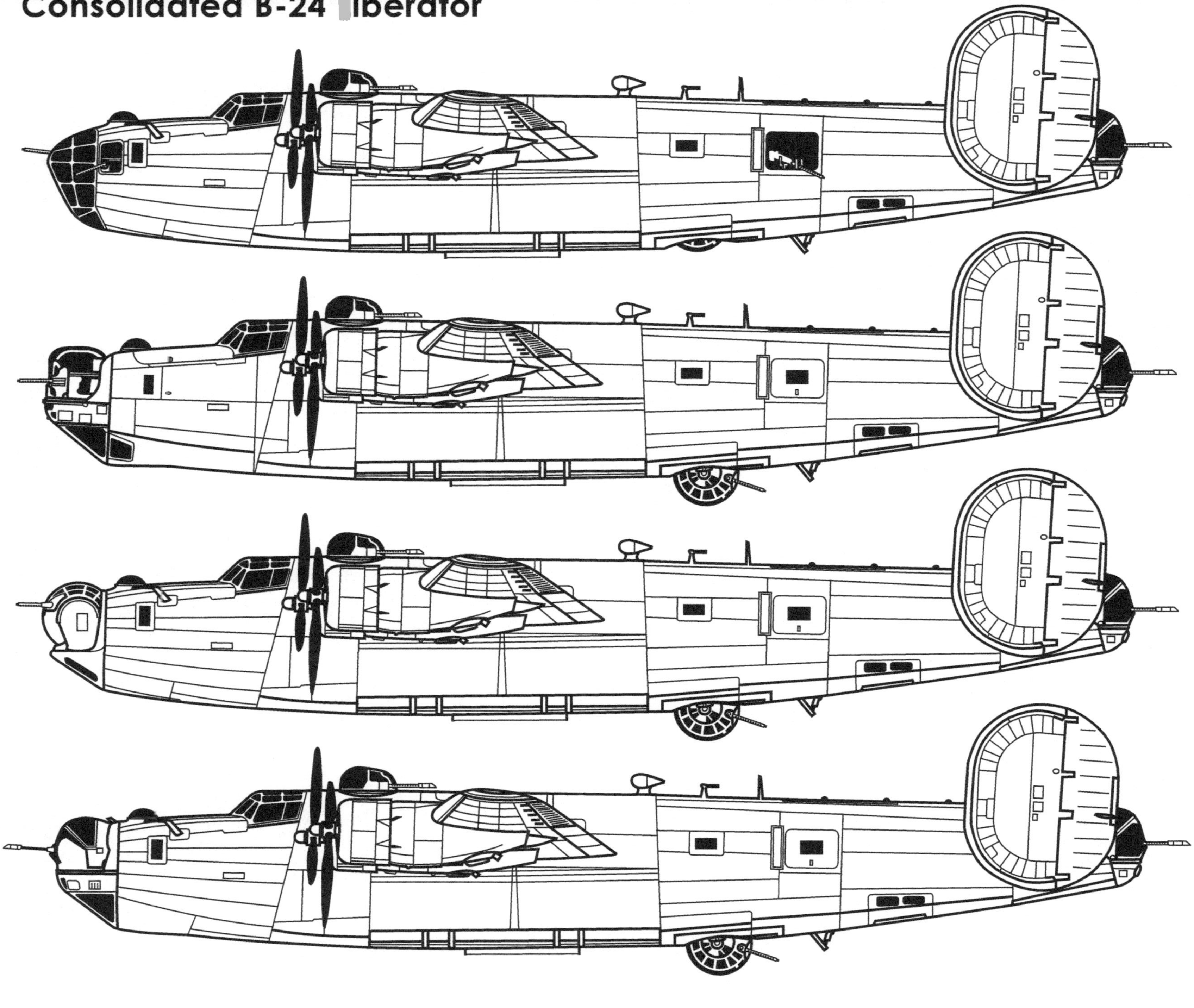

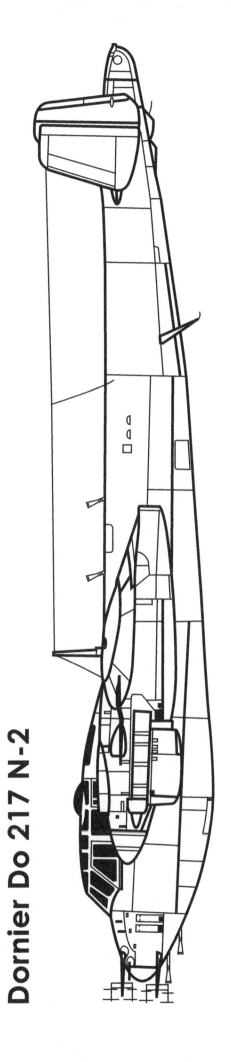

**Dornier Do 217 N-2**

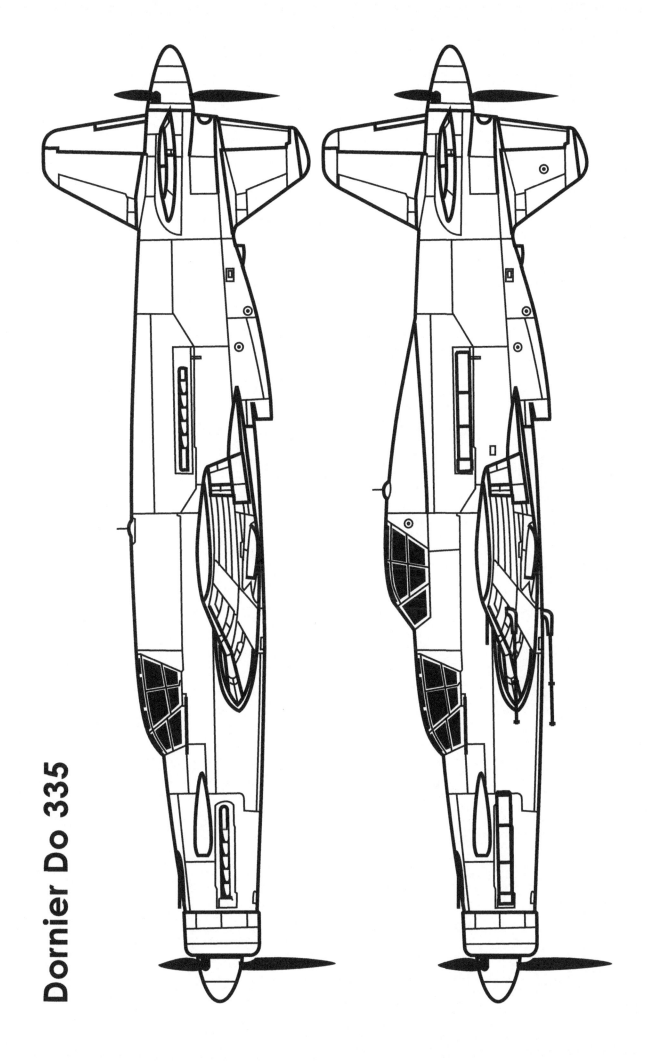

Dornier Do 335

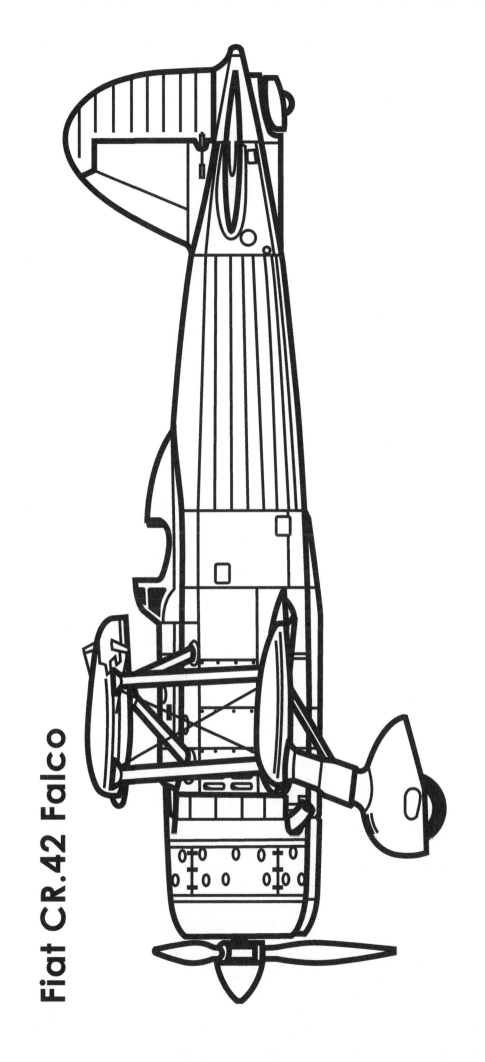

Fiat CR.42 Falco

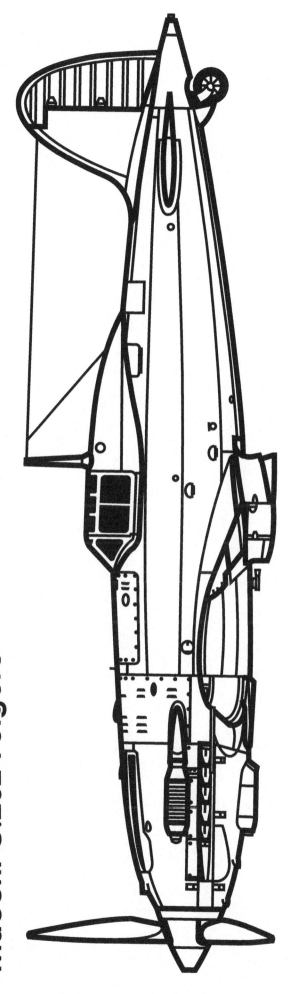

Macchi C.202 Folgore

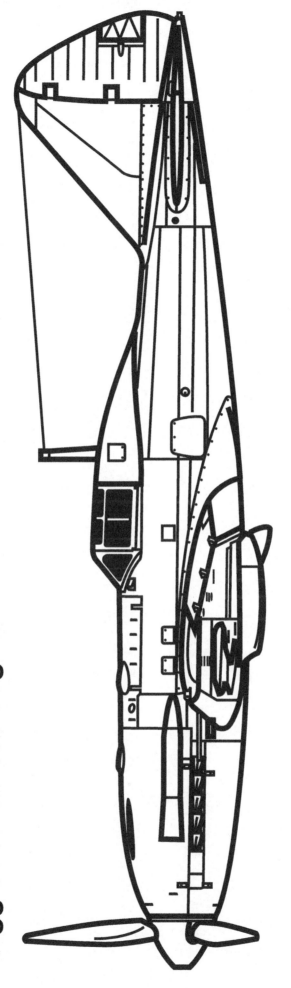

Reggiane Re.2005 Sagittario

Ilyushin Il-2 Shturmovik

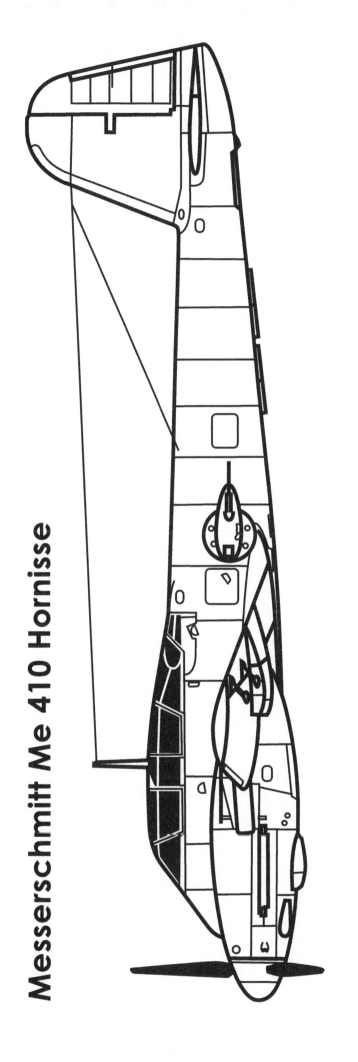

Messerschmitt Me 410 Hornisse

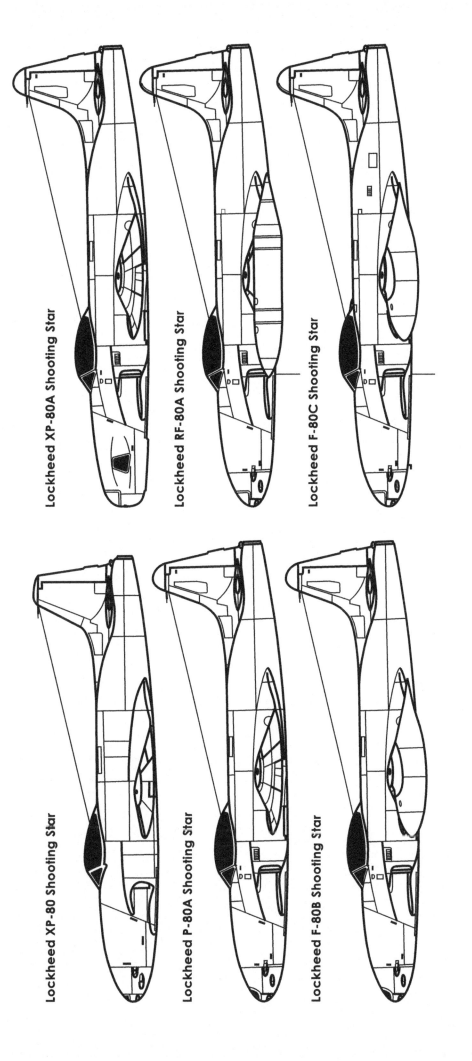

Lockheed XP-80A Shooting Star

Lockheed RF-80A Shooting Star

Lockheed F-80C Shooting Star

Lockheed XP-80 Shooting Star

Lockheed P-80A Shooting Star

Lockheed F-80B Shooting Star

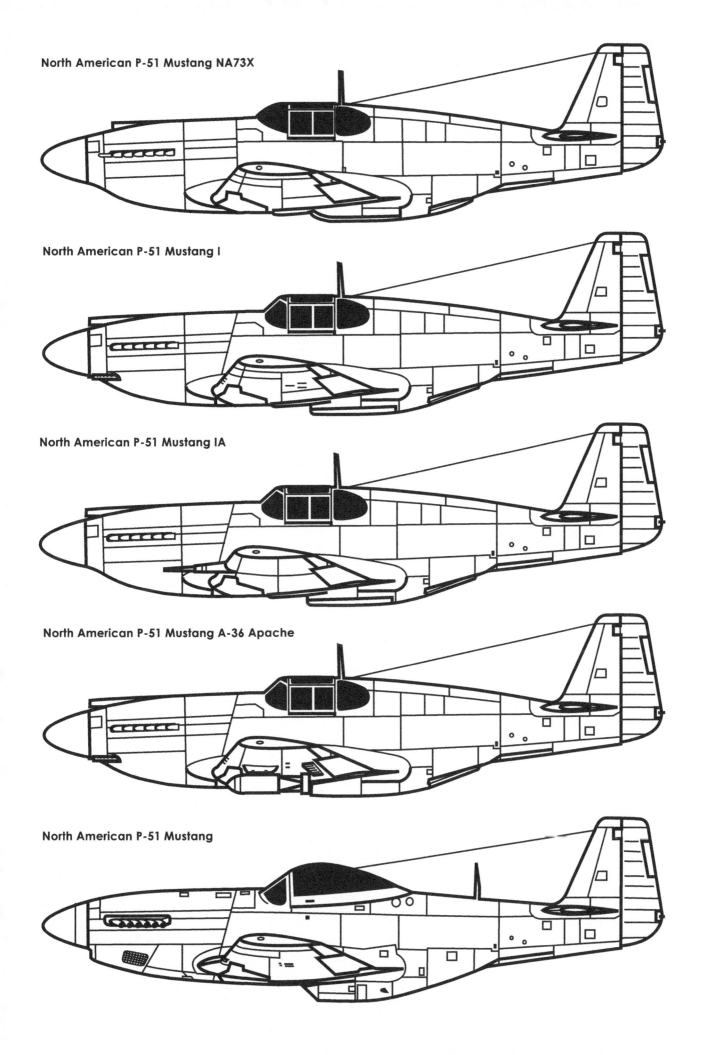

North American P-51 Mustang NA73X

North American P-51 Mustang I

North American P-51 Mustang IA

North American P-51 Mustang A-36 Apache

North American P-51 Mustang

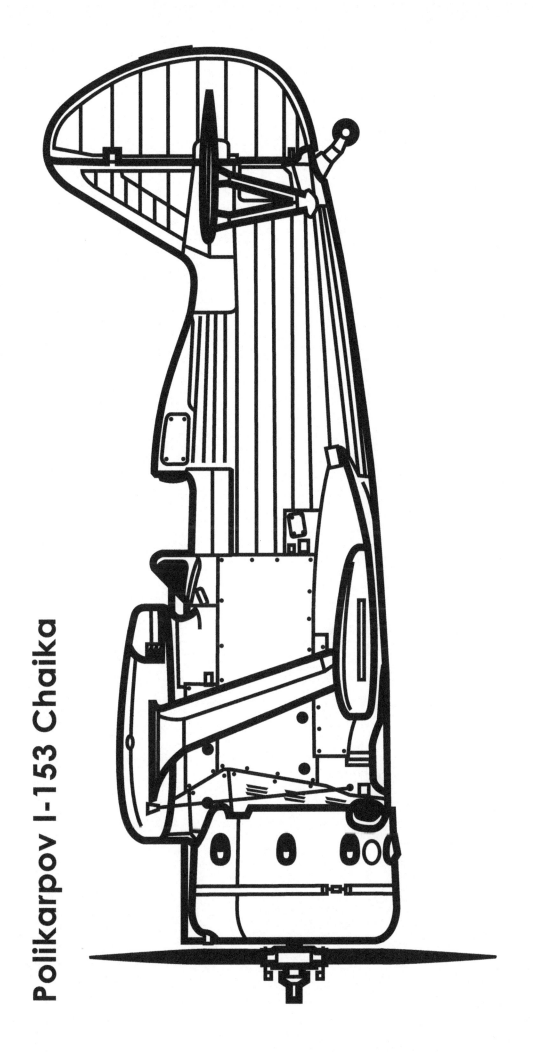

Polikarpov I-153 Chaika

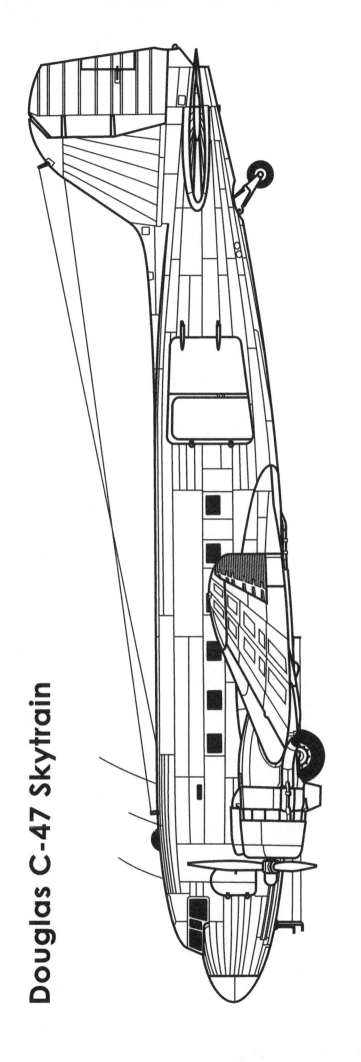

Douglas C-47 Skytrain

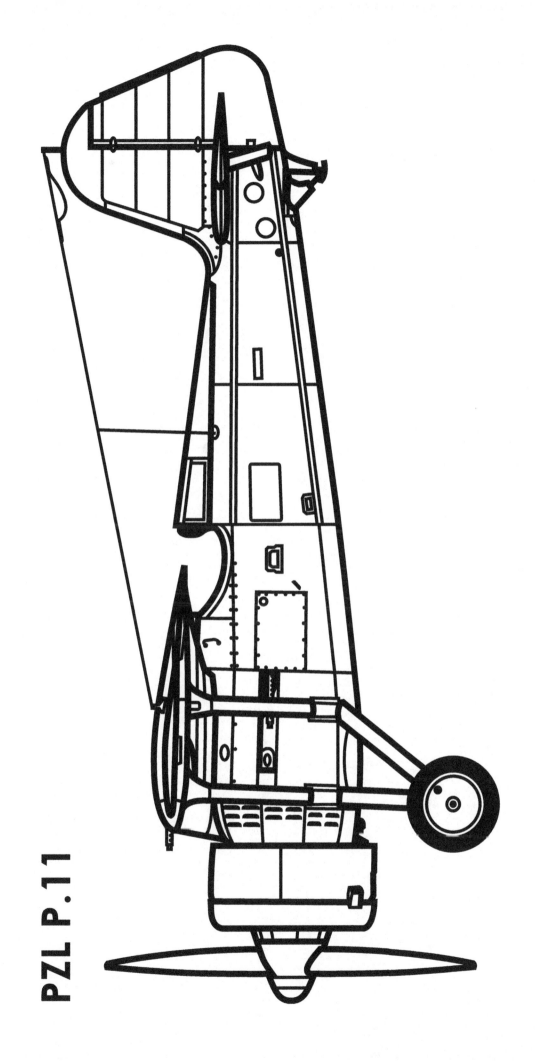

PZL P.11

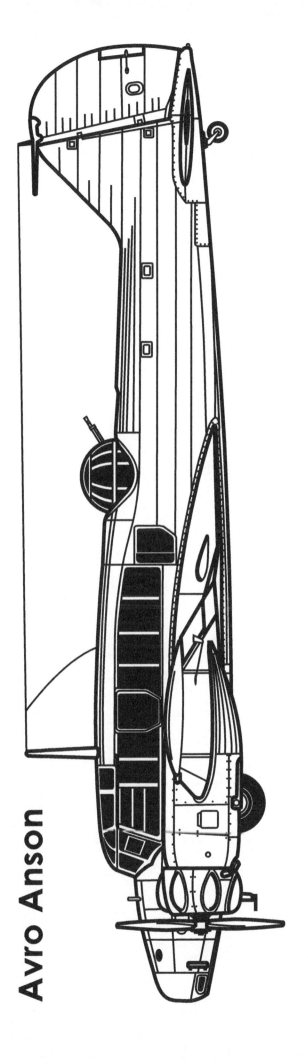

Avro Anson

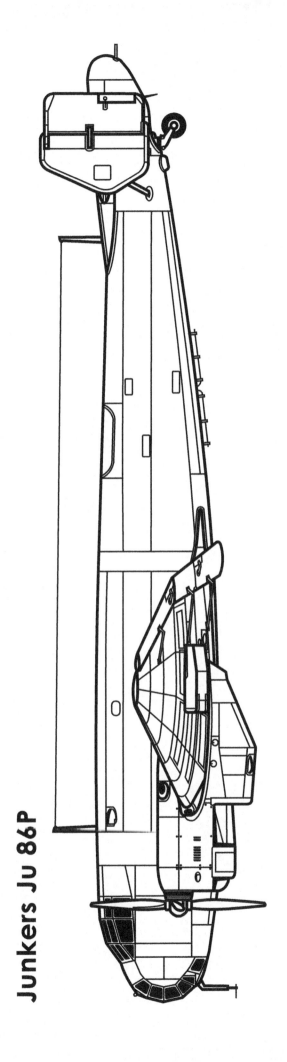

Junkers Ju 86P

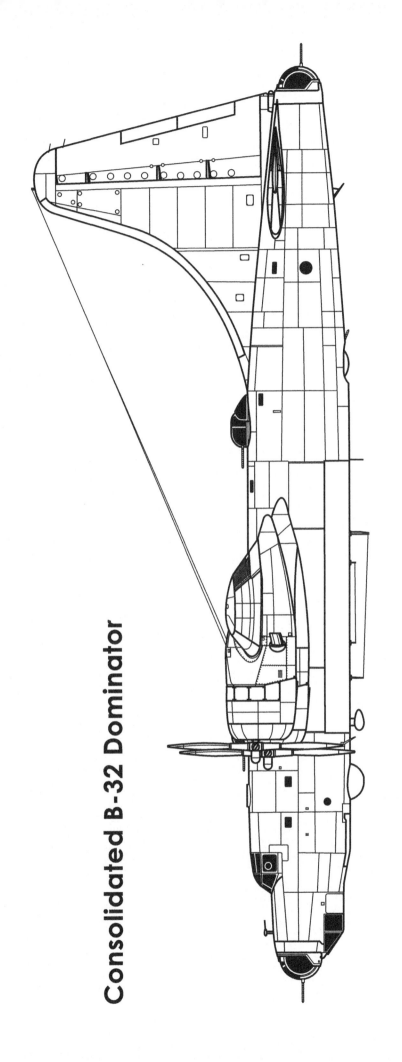

Consolidated B-32 Dominator

Made in the USA
Las Vegas, NV
01 May 2024

89372349R00090